STRONG STAFF, STRONG STUDENTS

professional development in schools and youth programs

ANGELA JERABEK, MS, AND NANCY TELLETT-ROYCE

SEARCH
INSTITUTE
PRESS

Strong Staff, Strong Students: Professional Development in Schools and Youth Programs
Angela Jerabek, MS, and Nancy Tellett-Royce

The following are registered trademarks of Search Institute: Search Institute®, Developmental Assets®, and

HEALTHY COMMUNITIES · HEALTHY YOUTH®

Search Institute Press, Minneapolis, MN
Copyright © 2010 by Search Institute

At the time of publication, all facts and figures cited herein are the most current available; all telephone numbers, addresses, and Web site URLs are accurate and active; all publications, organizations, Web sites, and other resources exist as described in this book; and all efforts have been made to verify them. The authors and Search Institute make no warranty or guarantee concerning the information and materials given out by organizations or content found at Web sites that are cited herein, and we are not responsible for any changes that occur after this book's publication. If you find an error or believe that a resource listed herein is not as described, please contact Client Services at Search Institute.

10 9 8 7 6 5 4 3 2 1
Printed on acid-free paper in the United States of America

Search Institute
615 First Avenue Northeast, Suite 125
Minneapolis, MN 55413
www.search-institute.org
612-376-8955 • 877-240-7251

ISBN-13: 978-1-57482-276-2

LIBRARY OF CONGRESS
CATALOGING-IN-PUBLICATION DATA
Jerabek, Angela.
    Strong staff, strong students : professional development in schools and youth programs / Angela Jerabek and Nancy Tellett-Royce.
        p. cm.
Includes index.
ISBN-13: 978-1-57482-276-2 (pbk. : alk. paper)
ISBN-10: 1-57482-276-4 (pbk. : alk. paper)
1. Teachers--In-service training. 2. Reflective teaching. 3. Mentoring in education. I. Tellett-Royce, Nancy. II. Title.
    LB1731.J435 2010
    370.71'55--dc22
                                    2010022295

CREDITS
Editor: Kate Brielmaier
Book Design: Jeenee Lee
Production Supervisor: Mary Ellen Buscher

ABOUT SEARCH INSTITUTE PRESS
Search Institute Press is a division of Search Institute, a nonprofit organization that offers leadership, knowledge, and resources to promote positive youth development. Our mission at Search Institute Press is to provide practical and hope-filled resources to help create a world in which all young people thrive. Our products are embedded in research, and the 40 Developmental Assets®—qualities, experiences, and relationships youth need to succeed—are a central focus of our resources. Our logo, the SIP flower, is a symbol of the thriving and healthy growth young people experience when they have an abundance of assets in their lives.

Contents

Introduction

Staff Development and the Developmental Assets

Imagine a world where all young people experienced a network of three to five caring adults as they were growing up. Who would these five be? Would you or your staff be among them?

When Search Institute has surveyed young people or asked them those questions in our trainings, they frequently name a parent, a teacher, a coach, a youth worker.

At first blush this seems encouraging—so many types of adults with the potential to be part of that network of support for our young people. But in Search Institute's survey work in the United States, only 43 percent of youth in grades 6 through 12 say that they receive support from three or more nonparent adults. That translates to just slightly more than two out of every five young people. Or if you like to think about the big picture, that percentage represents about 12 million teens who do not experience this basic web of support that research shows is important in contributing to their healthy development.

For those of us who work with young people in educational or programmatic settings, this finding is a call to action. In school after school, we have seen staff test this lack of supportive adults in a very simple way. Before a staff meeting, all the students' names are posted on the wall of the gym or cafeteria. All staff members are given stickers to place by the names of any students they know well enough to start a brief conversation with them if they saw them outside school. From the schools that have reported their results back to us, we have heard that typically, about a quarter of the students have many stickers by their names. Another quarter or so have one or two stickers. And nearly half have no stickers at all. No adult employed in that school "knows" those students.

Search Institute is working to change this situation. An independent, nonprofit, nonsectarian organization, Search Institute has developed a framework called the Developmental Assets®, grounded in research on child and adolescent development, risk prevention, and resiliency. The assets represent the relationships, opportunities, and personal qualities that young people need to avoid risks and to succeed in life.

This book is designed to offer the staff person or committee charged with professional development a set of activities, tools, and strategies that will support all staff members in expanding their knowledge of the Developmental Assets, increasing their abilities to create an asset-rich environment, and strengthening skills to provide the supportive relationships that young people need. It also suggests how to "bundle" these options in ways that can strengthen capacity over time.

What Are the Developmental Assets?

The 40 Developmental Assets describe qualities and experiences that are crucial to positive youth development. They range from external supports like a caring school climate and positive family communication to internal characteristics such as school engagement and a sense of purpose.

Search Institute has done extensive research, reviewing more than 1,200 studies from major bodies of literature, including prevention, resilience, and adolescent development, to identify what young people need to thrive. Institute researchers have documented that young people who are developmentally healthy, whether they come from the poorest or the wealthiest environments and from diverse ethnic and cultural groups, have certain meaningful elements in their lives. Researchers identified eight categories that describe these elements:

- The solid presence of **support** from others;
- A feeling of **empowerment**;
- A clear understanding of **boundaries and expectations**;
- Varied opportunities for **constructive use of time**;
- A strong **commitment to learning**;
- An appreciation of **positive values**;
- Sound **social competencies**; and
- A personal sense of **positive identity**.[1, 2]

Moreover, research conducted by Search Institute consistently shows that the strengths described within these categories provide a solid foundation for positive development and academic success, and that their presence helps protect youth from engaging in risky behavior and promotes youth acting in productive ways. The data

1. Peter C. Scales and Nancy Leffert, *Developmental Assets: A Synthesis of the Scientific Research on Adolescent Development*, 2nd ed. (Minneapolis: Search Institute, 2004).
2. Peter C. Scales, Arturo Sesma Jr., and Brent Bolstrom, *Coming into Their Own: How Developmental Assets Promote Positive Growth in Middle Childhood* (Minneapolis: Search Institute, 2004).

The Power of Assets

On one level, the 40 Developmental Assets represent common wisdom about the kinds of positive experiences and characteristics that young people need and deserve. But their value extends further. Surveys of more than 2 million young people in grades 6–12 have shown that assets are powerful influences on adolescent behavior. (The following numbers reflect 2003 data from 148,189 young people in 202 communities.) Regardless of the gender, ethnic heritage, economic situation, or geographic location of the youth surveyed, these assets promote positive behaviors and attitudes and help protect young people from many different problem behaviors.

0–10 ASSETS   11–20 ASSETS   21–30 ASSETS   31–40 ASSETS

FIGURE 1: PROMOTING POSITIVE BEHAVIORS AND ATTITUDES

Search Institute research shows that the more assets students report having, the more likely they also are to report the following patterns of thriving behavior:

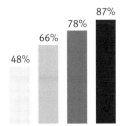

Exhibits Leadership
Has been a leader of an organization or group in the past 12 months.

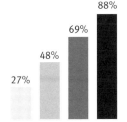

Maintains Good Health
Takes good care of body (such as eating foods that are healthy and exercising regularly).

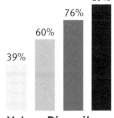

Values Diversity
Thinks it is important to get to know people of other racial/ethnic groups.

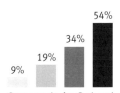

Succeeds in School
Gets mostly As on report card (an admittedly high standard).

FIGURE 2: PROTECTING YOUTH FROM HIGH-RISK BEHAVIORS

Assets not only promote positive behaviors—they also protect young people. The more assets a young person reports having, the less likely she is to make harmful or unhealthy choices. (Note that these definitions are set rather high, suggesting ongoing problems rather than experimentation.)

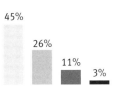

Problem Alcohol Use
Has used alcohol three or more times in the past 30 days or got drunk once or more in the past two weeks.

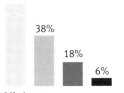

Violence
Has engaged in three or more acts of fighting, hitting, injuring a person, carrying a weapon, or threatening physical harm in the past 12 months.

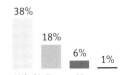

Illicit Drug Use
Used illicit drugs (marijuana, cocaine, LSD, PCP or angel dust, heroin, or amphetamines) three or more times in the past 12 months.

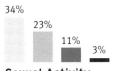

Sexual Activity
Has had sexual intercourse three or more times in lifetime.

The Framework of 40 Developmental Assets® for Adolescents

Search Institute has identified the following building blocks of healthy development that help young people grow up healthy, caring, and responsible.

EXTERNAL ASSETS

Support

1. **Family Support**
Family life provides high levels of love and support.

2. **Positive Family Communication**
Young person and her or his parent(s) communicate positively, and young person is willing to seek advice and counsel from parent(s).

3. **Other Adult Relationships**
Young person receives support from three or more nonparent adults.

4. **Caring Neighborhood**
Young person experiences caring neighbors.

5. **Caring School Climate**
School provides a caring, encouraging environment.

6. **Parent Involvement in Schooling**
Parent(s) are actively involved in helping young person succeed in school.

Empowerment

7. **Community Values Youth**
Young person perceives that adults in the community value youth.

8. **Youth as Resources**
Young people are given useful roles in the community.

9. **Service to Others**
Young person serves in the community one hour or more per week.

10. **Safety**—Young person feels safe at home, at school, and in the neighborhood.

Boundaries and Expectations

11. **Family Boundaries**
Family has clear rules and consequences and monitors the young person's whereabouts.

12. **School Boundaries**
School provides clear rules and consequences.

13. **Neighborhood Boundaries**
Neighbors take responsibility for monitoring young people's behavior.

14. **Adult Role Models**
Parent(s) and other adults model positive, responsible behavior.

15. **Positive Peer Influence**
Young person's best friends model responsible behavior.

16. **High Expectations**
Both parent(s) and teachers encourage the young person to do well.

Constructive Use of Time

17. **Creative Activities**
Young person spends three or more hours per week in lessons or practice in music, theater, or other arts.

18. **Youth Programs**
Young person spends three or more hours per week in sports, clubs, or organizations at school and/or in the community.

19. **Religious Community**
Young person spends one or more hours per week in activities in a religious institution.

20. **Time at Home**
Young person is out with friends "with nothing special to do" two or fewer nights per week.

INTERNAL ASSETS

Commitment to Learning

21. *Achievement Motivation*
Young person is motivated to do well in school.

22. *School Engagement*
Young person is actively engaged in learning.

23. *Homework*
Young person reports doing at least one hour of homework every school day.

24. *Bonding to School*
Young person cares about her or his school.

25. *Reading for Pleasure*
Young person reads for pleasure three or more hours per week.

Positive Values

26. *Caring*
Young person places high value on helping other people.

27. *Equality and Social Justice*
Young person places high value on promoting equality and reducing hunger and poverty.

28. *Integrity*
Young person acts on convictions and stands up for her or his beliefs.

29. *Honesty*
Young person "tells the truth even when it is not easy."

30. *Responsibility*
Young person accepts and takes personal responsibility.

31. *Restraint*
Young person believes it is important not to be sexually active or to use alcohol or other drugs.

Social Competencies

32. *Planning and Decision Making*
Young person knows how to plan ahead and make choices.

33. *Interpersonal Competence*
Young person has empathy, sensitivity, and friendship skills.

34. *Cultural Competence*—Young person has knowledge of and comfort with people of different cultural/racial/ethnic backgrounds.

35. *Resistance Skills*
Young person can resist negative peer pressure and dangerous situations.

36. *Peaceful Conflict Resolution*
Young person seeks to resolve conflict nonviolently.

Positive Identity

37. *Personal Power*
Young person feels he or she has control over "things that happen to me."

38. *Self-Esteem*
Young person reports having a high self-esteem.

39. *Sense of Purpose*
Young person reports that "my life has a purpose."

40. *Positive View of Personal Future*
Young person is optimistic about her or his personal future.

consistently show that the power of assets is cumulative: the more assets young people report experiencing, the more apt they are to succeed in school and live positive lives, and the less likely they are to participate in high-risk behaviors such as drug use, violence, and early sexual activity.

About This Book

Strong Staff, Strong Students has been written because classrooms and out-of-school programs are places where young people spend a great deal of time, and staff in these settings are critical role models and empowerment agents in their lives. The better they are equipped for this work, the more effective they can be.

It has also been written in response to many requests over the years for activities that can be used in staff meetings, or resources that can be built into professional development programs. This book is an effort to respond to those requests in a systematic way.

Section I discusses some issues that face adults who lead staff development efforts and offers ways to deal with them. Chapter 1 includes information on adult learning styles and changing mindsets, suggestions for dealing with common roadblocks, and best practices for creating an effective staff development program. Chapter 2 covers information on incorporating the Developmental Assets into your staff development program.

Section II provides staff development activities and materials. Chapter 3 introduces staff to the Developmental Assets with a PowerPoint presentation, while Chapter 4 offers activities and exercises designed for staff meetings and professional learning communities (PLCs). These ideas will help your staff strengthen and deepen their understanding of the Developmental Assets using inventories, discussion, and reflection questions. Chapter 5 includes physical materials to help keep the assets at the forefront of staff awareness. Posters, wallet cards, and handouts all combine to create constant reminders that one goal for staff is to discover and build assets.

Finally, Section III offers ideas on putting all these elements together to build a comprehensive and cohesive staff development plan. Chapter 6 provides suggested groupings of the materials found in the previous chapters and a sample calendar that gives an example of how you might put a plan together.

Every school and youth-serving organization is filled with adults who care about young people and take seriously their work in guiding the learning and development of children and teens. These adults have a crucial role to play in improving young people's odds for success. We hope the resources in this book help you further equip them for the important work they do.

One Final Note

While staff development activities will begin the work of deepening and broadening the use of the Developmental Assets framework and asset-building strategies, a focus on continuous improvement will drive the work further. It has been our experience that it can take one year or several years of staff development activities to lay the groundwork for asset building in an organization. While follow-on activities—including site walk-throughs, activity observations, staff and youth surveys, and periodic reviews of the data collected in these ways—are outside the scope of this book, it is important to note that they will further enhance the effectiveness of asset-building efforts.

Search Institute has created a training, *Good to Great,* that covers these continuous improvement strategies and can be a useful next step to deepening effectiveness.

SECTION I

STAFF DEVELOPMENT THEORY

Chapter 1

Issues in Staff Development

Starting or maintaining a staff development program can be a challenge. Even when you account for the expected barriers, such as time constraints, funding limitations, and staff buy-in, unexpected obstacles can appear in your path without warning. This chapter provides a solid foundation, based on recent research, to help you discover the best ways to tailor your staff development program to your staff's needs. It also looks at specific obstacles to staff development and offers ways to overcome them. Finally, it suggests strategies to help you quickly and easily integrate aspects of the Developmental Assets into your staff development program—before you even have your first meeting.

What Is Staff Development?

"Staff development" is a phrase that has been used to describe everything from informal after-school gatherings, to formal lectures where staff passively receive information, to professional learning community activities in which staff take charge of much of their own learning.

For the purposes of this book, we are defining staff development as a constellation of actions, carried out over time, that include high-quality trainings, and activities and resources that reinforce and expand on concepts covered in the trainings. Staff development includes both formal and informal opportunities for practice so that staff members can improve their skills and become more effective asset builders. It likewise requires time for discussion and reflection by staff so that they can bring their own best ideas to bear on how to create an asset-rich environment for young people. We are also mindful that staff development includes providing the structural and leadership supports necessary for effective implementation.

This book is intended to complement the National Staff Development Council (NSDC) Standards for Staff Development, which are organized into three categories:

- **CONTEXT:** the organization or system within which the learning will take place, with some contexts being more supportive of that learning than others. A supportive context, in this book, includes leadership committed to embedding the Developmental Assets and asset-building strategies throughout the programs and practices of the building, as well as committing resources and adequate time during the workday for staff development activities to take place.

- **PROCESS:** the ways in which staff development activities are carried out. Ideally, staff development is a thoughtful process, with key components mapped out in advance. This process also includes an emphasis on collaborative skills and developing the group. It is important to remember that there is an initiation phase in which new content and practices are introduced, but there are also implementation and institutionalization phases that allow for ongoing practice, until behaviors shift from occasional to habitual and key strategies finally become part of the organization's culture. For this to happen, there need to be ways to measure impact and tie asset building to the overall mission of the organization.

- **CONTENT:** the knowledge base and skills that staff members need to have or acquire to be effective. While the NSDC identifies many core content standards, most of which support asset-building efforts (diversity, service-learning, high expectations, family involvement, and so on), this book will focus on knowledge and skills that pertain to the Developmental Assets.[1]

What Researchers Tell Us about Ourselves

In your job as an educator or youth worker, you probably pay a lot of attention to the ways in which kids learn best, changing activities to keep things interesting and making sure you reinforce lessons over time to build skills. Math is a good example: every skill a child learns is repeated again and again, and eventually other skills that build on those first exercises are introduced. You have to vary the lessons to keep children from getting bored, and you have to find ways to apply the concepts to the real world.

---

1. National Staff Development Council, *National Staff Development Council's Standards for Staff Development: Middle Level Edition* (Oxford, OH: National Staff Development Council, 1994).

But when it comes to adult learning, we forget that the same approach applies to us. When many of us think about professional development or staff development, we immediately think of providing information in the context of a training—a "one and done" program that introduces new ideas but doesn't necessarily provide any reinforcement in day-to-day life. It's important that trainings not only present specific knowledge and skills but also show those skills in action and provide a context for using them.

The Power of Reinforcement

In research carried out by IBM and later replicated by the UK post office, people were divided into three groups. Each group was taught the same task using three different approaches. The first group was told the information about how to do a task. The second group was both told the information and shown how to do the task. The third group was told the information, was shown how to do the task, and then practiced doing the task. Members of each group were retested three weeks, and then three months, after the initial instruction to see whether they could still perform the task.

The results are shown in the table below:[2]

TASK	TOLD	TOLD AND SHOWN	TOLD, SHOWN, PRACTICED
Recall after 3 weeks	70%	72%	85%
Recall after 3 months	10%	32%	65%

You can see that those who were not only told about and shown but also given an opportunity to practice the task did much better when they were retested in three weeks than those who were only told about the task, or even those who were told about and shown the task. The difference that was found when groups were retested at three months is even more pronounced. Clearly, reinforcement of a task or a concept pays off in the long term.

In an example a little closer to our topic, Keith Pattinson, formerly the associate national director of the Boys and Girls Clubs of Canada and a regular presenter on the Developmental Assets to audiences across Canada and the United States, worked with an evaluator who followed up on introductory presentations Keith made in five communities across British Columbia. Two hundred and eighteen participants completed pre- and post-training questionnaires. Of those participants, 41 volunteered

---

2. John Whitmore, *Coaching for Performance*, 3rd ed. (London: Nicholas Brealey Publishing, 2002), 22.

to take part in phone interviews three months later, while 38 also agreed to be interviewed six months after the workshops. The workshops included information about the Developmental Assets, time to reflect on asset builders in participants' own lives, and an exercise that invited them to identify specific acts of asset building they could begin to do personally. Below are four findings from this small evaluation:

- Participants' recollections of the presenter's delivery and specific framework elements faded over time, which you would probably expect to be the case.

- Participants' recollections of the link between assets and healthy development and the categories of assets grew over time, with participants being most likely to remember the asset category of "Support."

- At six months, more than half the respondents reported that they had reverted to non-asset-building habits, particularly if they were with other adults who did not practice asset building.

- Six months after the training, 80 percent said they wanted additional support to reinforce or further develop their asset-building efforts.[3]

So as you create your professional development strategies for asset building, remember that training is a fine place to start but is not sufficient to anchor deep behavior change over time. For that reason, while we have included an introductory script and PowerPoint slides to use when you are providing basic information about the Developmental Assets, as well as a series of information sheets that can reinforce the content, we also include activities that will help you embed asset-building practices in your setting through repeated exposure, practice, and reflection over time.

The Four Stages of Learning

John Whitmore presents a useful way to think about the stages of the learning cycle. He breaks it into four stages:

1. **Unconscious incompetence:** We're unaware that we don't know something.

2. **Conscious incompetence:** We become aware that we don't know something, or can't perform it well.

---

3. Angela Matheson, "Asset Building: Evaluating the Process . . . Measuring the Outcomes." Prepared for the Boys and Girls Clubs of British Columbia, Community Mobilization Program, National Crime Prevention Centre, 2002 (unpublished document).

3. **Conscious competence:** We're aware that we are mastering something, but need to concentrate in order to make the necessary changes.

4. **Unconscious competence:** We are able to perform a new task without thinking about it because we have achieved a degree of mastery.[4]

While not everyone starts at stage 1, **unconscious incompetence,** most of us have at least a few areas where we are unconscious of our incompetence. We don't know what we don't know and therefore have no reason to change our behavior. Sometimes this is because we have preconceptions about how easy a task is, and sometimes it is because we don't know there is a better way.

To run through the four stages, let's use the example of learning to drive a car. In this first stage, unconscious incompetence, we haven't yet tried to drive a car, and from our casual observation of people driving while we sit in the passenger seat, it doesn't seem very difficult at all. Only when we want to learn how to drive do we move toward stage 2.

Stage 2 occurs when we become aware of what we can't do or don't know. We are **conscious** of our **incompetence.** When we take our first turn behind the wheel of a car, we are suddenly aware of having to do too many tasks, all of which must be coordinated, in too little time. "Look both ways, put in the clutch, shift into first gear, let up the clutch, apply the gas, don't forget to look again. Repeat the cycle to move into second and then third gear." We find the process nerve-racking and we both need the coaching we receive and are frustrated by it at the same time. We may notice physical cues that we are in this stage: our shoulders may ache, or perhaps we

---

4. Whitmore, *Coaching for Performance*, 102–7.

experience headaches more often. During stage 2 we need support and sometimes some help in selecting the right skills to work on or specific strategies we can try. We feel awkward as we try, consciously, to build the new skills. Practice, practice, and more practice eventually can help us move to the next stage.

Stage 3 is **conscious competence.** In this stage we become aware of everything coming together. We know what we have to do and we do it with less effort and more grace. The car starts, we move through the gears, we attend to traffic around us, we feel on top of our game. We are still paying close attention, but the actions require less effort and are less stressful. In a work setting, external observations and reviews can help us keep our momentum going in this stage.

Through conscious and ongoing practice we can move into stage 4, **unconscious competence.** Our learned behaviors have become habits and we don't consciously think about the steps we are taking. Further practice continues to improve our skills. One challenge that crops up here, however, is when someone who is unconsciously competent at a task must explain what he or she actually does to someone who is trying to learn the behavior. Sometimes this process allows individuals to reflect on their practice in new ways and deepen their competence. But there are many examples, particularly in the area of sports, of someone trying to bring the steps back into conscious focus only to make them more difficult to perform. Think of the challenge of trying to verbalize every move we make to shoot a free throw, or trying to explain how to tie a necktie.

To apply this to asset building in our professional lives, most of us may assume we do a fairly good job of interacting with the young people in our classroom or program. Then perhaps an overheard remark made by a student or an observation made by a colleague, or a nagging feeling that we are just not getting through to a particular student moves us to consider whether there is some skill we need to sharpen in order to achieve better results. Another case might be when we observe a professional using a new technique and realize that it might apply to our practice as well.

As we begin to reflect on our own behaviors, or invite and listen to the observations of a trusted colleague, we may feel the same tension we felt when we were learning to drive, until we master a few key steps and begin feeling more at home with this new set of skills.

Both practice and positive results help us stay the course and continue to work on our new skills. Having colleagues who are working on the same skills and talking about the learning process can make this stage more enjoyable and more productive. At some point the new skills become habits, making way for our attention to turn in a new direction and giving us the opportunity to identify other skills yet to be developed.

Several interesting things can happen as we personally go through this cycle. If we already have made habits of some of the skills involved in asset building, working with colleagues gives us a way to bring those skills back into our conscious mind, which gives us an opportunity to deepen them. If we start using new asset-building skills and strategies, we may be rewarded by deeper relationships with both our students and our colleagues. (Asset building isn't just for kids, after all.) And in our struggles with ourselves as we go through stage 2, conscious incompetence, we may gain a new appreciation for the struggles our students go through on their own learning journeys.

Our hope is that this resource will help professionals who are new to asset building learn a new set of skills that will improve their effectiveness, and that the activities in this book will help seasoned asset builders lead their colleagues into deepening those skills.

Mindset

World-renowned Stanford University psychologist Carol Dweck has named a powerful factor in learning—an individual's mindset. Dweck's work reveals that ability and talent are only small pieces of the story of an individual's success. Her research focuses on how perception of ourselves (both conscious and unconscious) significantly influences our personality and our openness to change. She asserts that our mindset is as important as our natural abilities and talents in achieving success. The lens of mindset brings into clarity why some individuals achieve greatness in science, arts, sports, business, and other areas, and also potentially explains the "would have beens."[5]

Alfred Binet, the father of the IQ assessment, asserted that it is not always the people who start out the smartest who end up the smartest. This phenomenon happens all the time in schools and often amazes skeptical teachers: some students come into high school in grade 9 with no hint that they will graduate as tremendous leaders with incredible opportunities before them; others start grade 9 with résumés that indicate they will blaze new trails and break school records and yet, with all those indicators, they appear to just coast to graduation. Binet designed the IQ test to identify students who would benefit from programs to get students back on track, but he believed that the IQ test was a measurement of *change,* not fixed ability. Binet believed that although there were individual differences in children's abilities,

---

5. Carol Dweck, *Mindset: The New Psychology of Success* (New York: Ballantine, 2007).

experiences could change a child's intelligence. The same thing is true for adults: new experiences can change intelligence. The question becomes, what changes their trajectories? Dweck's theory helps frame an explanation.

Dweck states that there are two mindsets: the **fixed mindset** and the **growth mindset.** A person with a fixed mindset believes that an individual's attributes—personality, intelligence, temperament—are finite and natural gifts. Often these are the people who are identified as "gifted" at a young age, and they often wear their title like a badge of honor. It is important to an individual with a fixed mindset to demonstrate these characteristics to the world, as she often perceives these qualities to be depictions of herself: "I am gifted . . . so I'd better look gifted." Fixed-mindset individuals can have an urgent need to prove themselves time and time again. An individual with a fixed mindset does not need to ask for help: she has natural talent, and natural talent does not require effort or help. Effort is for those who do not have natural gifts, and effort represents weakness. Fixed-mindset individuals often perceive that a key to success is ensuring that they are always demonstrating their gifts—effortlessly.

There is a huge downside to a fixed mindset. These individuals work very hard to protect their image, and taking risks is dangerous for them. If you try new things and you are not successful, what will others think? What will you think? Will you still be gifted?

Fixed-mindset individuals must have an excuse if things don't work out (it can't be that they are not capable); otherwise the label they proudly bear would be false. During the height of his career, tennis player John McEnroe appeared to have a fixed mindset. When pressure mounted and he wasn't successful, he always had an excuse. The sawdust he used to increase his grip on the racket would be too fine or too coarse; he was too hot or too cold; it was too noisy, too quiet: *he* was never the reason he lost. That risk would be too great—to admit that there was something he needed to work on. Often, a fixed-mindset individual's full potential is not realized because of self-imposed limitations.

People can be paralyzed by this mindset. The concerns associated with the fixed mindset ("Will I look stupid?" "What if I am wrong?" "What will the other students or staff think?") dominate their lives. Students resist taking honors courses because they fear they will receive lower grades than they would in standard courses: they consciously choose not to challenge themselves owing to the perceived risk involved in receiving less than an A. Adults choose not to participate in an activity at which they are not already skilled because they fear they will look foolish. Fixed-mindset individuals receive lots of validation and have many successes; they have been identified as "bright," "gifted," and "skilled," and they are reluctant to relinquish those titles by taking a risk.

The **growth mindset,** on the other hand, is based on the belief that individuals possess basic qualities that can be enhanced through motivation, effort, and education. It does not assert that anyone can become a genius, but it does insist that everyone can change and grow through effort. Growth-mindset individuals thrive on challenges: they are always seeking the next level.

There are many examples of successful athletes, academics, and artists who fall into this category. Mia Hamm, one of the greatest female soccer players of her time, states that she always tried to play with older, more skilled, and more experienced players in order to grow. She did not fear looking foolish—she wanted the challenge, the ability to grow.

Many accomplished individuals were considered to have no future in their chosen areas. Charles Darwin and Leo Tolstoy were both considered ordinary children, yet they clearly achieved exceptional things. Elvis Presley and Lucille Ball were advised not to pursue their dreams. Michael Jordan was cut from his high school basketball team. He wasn't a natural, but he may be the hardest-working athlete of our time. These individuals' skills may not have merited recognition at the time, but what wasn't taken into account was their potential to develop their skills and their capacity for growth.

Another notable difference between the growth mindset and the fixed mindset is the way individuals who have a growth mindset deal with adversity or setback. Jim Marshall, former defensive player for the Minnesota Vikings, is an excellent example of a growth mindset. In 1964, Marshall recovered a fumbled ball and ran it 67 yards for a touchdown . . . for the other team, the San Francisco 49ers. During halftime, he made a conscious decision, realizing he could either wallow in embarrassment or accept the mistake and move on. He played exceptionally well in the second half and contributed to his own team's victory.

Mindset affects not just your view of yourself but also your expectation of others. In school, mindset manifests itself in systemic ways as well as with individual students, staff, and parents. "Testing" into honors courses is a perfect example of how past performance and a fixed mindsct limit possibilities. Fixed mindset regularly influences interactions between staff and students, as students are questioned about the wisdom of attempting higher-level course work and cautioned about the ramifications of lower grade point averages. Students and families do need information to make educated decisions (hence the need to understand GPAs), but a love of learning and the quest for new challenges are lifelong skills that exemplify a growth mindset. A fixed mindset can create nonlearners if it is not carefully monitored.

A school counselor recounted the following story after learning about mindset:

This concept of mindset made me think of my grandmother Agnes Untiedt. My grandmother passed away last year at the age of 90. She was incredibly verbose and loved to talk about her family. When asked about her dozen grandchildren, she would brag about their most recent accomplishment, be it rolling over at 2 months, coloring a picture at 2 years of age, getting a job at 16, or completing a degree at age 40. She would always say, "He [or she] is all there, plus." I would always chuckle at this saying as I wondered: What was the "plus"? And how could we be all there . . . plus??? My grandma always saw the potential. She had a growth mindset, and she knew whatever she saw now was "the all there" but the "plus" was what was yet to come—and she knew it would!

The growth mindset can be a powerful force for change in a school and in students' lives. An administrator shared this wonderful illustration of mindset in a school setting during a staff meeting:

This past spring, as I was sitting in my office, I watched as a 9th-grade student was led in handcuffs to a police car. I was disappointed, as this was a student many staff had been working with and clearly he had made some poor decisions that day. I watched him being placed in the backseat of the police car and noted one of the school counselors running out to the car to speak to him. I was surprised, and after she came back inside I asked what had occurred. She told me she wanted to tell the student that he had been making some progress in his behavior and had been pulling his grades up, so this was a temporary setback. She wanted to tell him to stop in her office as soon as he was back and they would come up with a new plan.

The counselor clearly had a growth mindset and did not believe the school had seen all this student was capable of.

Mindset and the Developmental Assets

So how does Dweck's concept of growth and fixed mindsets fit with the Developmental Assets and staff development?

The social sciences traditionally have looked at young people in terms of a fixed mindset. They put youth into categories: socioeconomic status (high or low), neighborhood (high or low poverty, high or low violence), education level achieved by their parents (some high school, high school graduate, some college, college graduate), the absence or presence of one or both parents. None of these factors is under the control of a young person—but the presence of some combination of them will often lead adults around a young person to assume that these characteristics define the most likely outcomes for him or her. This is a fixed mindset.

Research on the Developmental Assets, and also research from the field of resiliency, tell us there is another way to view young people. The Developmental Assets name positive actions adults can take and opportunities they can provide to help a young person develop into a healthy, productive, responsible adult. One of the most important aspects of the Developmental Assets is that they are dependent on adults' viewing youth as having the capacity to change and grow in positive ways: it requires a growth mindset.

The asset-building process depends on young people's finding secure relationships with adults. These relationships provide them with the support and encouragement and the boundaries and expectations that lead to learning to think with a growth mindset. This growth mindset can give youth the tools they need to create positive, hope-filled futures for themselves: "I can change for the better with effort. I can develop the skills I need to be successful. People around me expect good things of me."

Dweck's work is particularly exciting because of the years she has spent identifying strategies to help individuals shift from a fixed to a growth mindset. For students, she has developed an online curriculum called Brainology (www.brainology .us/default.aspx) that helps youth move to a growth mindset, which is also a learning mindset. For a deeper understanding of Dweck's work, read *Mindset: The New Psychology of Success* (New York: Ballantine, 2007).

Changing Mindset

Sometimes, staff may hold a growth mindset about their students yet be stuck in a fixed mindset about themselves, or vice versa. If a staff person assumes he or she is a "natural" at working with youth, and already has all the competencies needed to do a job effectively, it can hamper the learning and practicing of new skills. It's a fixed mindset: "This feels awkward." "Why should I have to do this?" "I already know how to build relationships with young people." "I don't want other staff to see me fumble through this exercise."

To help staff take an initial step to moving toward or deepening a growth mindset, try the following activity.

Learning a New Mindset

Objective

To show staff how to recognize a fixed mindset and adjust it to a growth mindset.

It's not always easy to see how often we react with a fixed mindset. This exercise gives staff members a way to evaluate their reactions to a scenario, see whether those reactions are representative of a fixed mindset, and think of ways to turn them into new actions that use a growth mindset.

Time Required

10–20 minutes

Materials Needed

Learning a New Mindset handout (one for each participant)

Instructions

Distribute copies of the Learning a New Mindset handout and ask staff members to fill it out. When they are finished, lead a discussion about the results, focusing particularly on initial reactions to the "rejection" scenario and how unaware many people are of holding a "fixed" perspective.

Learning a New Mindset

Situation

Imagine that you have applied to a very competitive graduate program. You have not applied to any others. You feel confident in your abilities and assume you are going to be accepted—but then you learn the graduate program has rejected you.

Fixed Mindset Reaction

List three reasons why the rejection does not reflect personally on you. For example: The graduate program had an incredibly large talent pool to draw on.

At this point, someone with a fixed mindset may find doubts creeping in: "Maybe my work was ordinary?" "Maybe I'm not really cut out for graduate school?" But then that person talks him- or herself back into a more flattering self-image, denying doubts and reaffirming all the reasons the rejection was out of his or her control—the reasons you listed above. That is where he or she stops, self-esteem once again intact. But for a person with a growth mindset, this is just the beginning.

Growth Mindset Step

Review your goal and what steps you could take or information you could gather to keep moving toward it.

The key in the growth mindset is to then make one or more of these steps as vivid as possible so that you're encouraged and motivated to actually take the step. Select one of the steps you listed. Detail what you would do to follow through on that one step. Paint a vivid picture. Give it a time line.

If you have ever taught a lesson on planning and decision making, those growth-mindset steps will sound familiar: identify your goal, list the steps needed to reach that goal, and break each step into manageable parts.

For most of us, even if we know this in our heads, it is a challenge to follow through. This is why practice and reinforcement are important tools. There is comfort in staying put: even if we aren't where we want to be, at least the terrain is familiar. Shifting to a growth mindset invites us to be open to change—which can be scary, but also gives us the tools we need to work toward our goals.

Common Obstacles to Staff Development—and Some Solutions

Every school and youth program has its own character and "feel"—and its own unique challenges. There are, however, some roadblocks common to every staff development program.

Staff Buy-in

Time and time again, staff buy-in is listed as a significant barrier to professional development, particularly among veteran staff. The most experienced staff often teach the honors-level courses that typically have the smallest class sizes, with motivated and high-achieving students. Many times these teachers do not see a need for change, and they may be the leaders in the building.

Question: How can I engage a staff that does not perceive a problem?

Answer: A successful strategy to address a staff engagement barrier is to present staff with real and motivating data to elicit their participation.

It is necessary to provide background information on Developmental Assets—particularly data on their effectiveness. The handout on page 7, The Power of Assets, is based on survey results from nearly 150,000 students and shows a clear correlation between the number of assets a student reports having and his or her academic success.

To motivate these key leaders, data should be personalized to their school and pertain to their students. When staff members see the results of surveys that originate from their own school, they are even more likely to respond to staff development programs. Search Institute offers several surveys that help administrators and staff measure the health of their school, including the *Profiles of Student Life: Attitudes and Behaviors* survey, which measures the 40 Developmental Assets, as well as the Four Core Measures required for federal grants. You can find out more at search-institute.org/survey-services.

You can create your own surveys using online tools such as Survey Monkey (surveymonkey.com) and similar programs. Survey Monkey is a tool that organizations can use for minimal cost that collects data confidentially and then synthesizes the results. It can be used for multiple populations (staff, students, parents), and questions can be individualized based on needs (staff climate, student needs, leadership). The reporting and discussion of data are critical to staff engagement. The data should be delivered from reputable sources. Specific data that reflect the staff you are working with are very helpful in promoting staff buy-in.

Question: How do we engage all staff when a small staff group is leading the charge?

Answer: A successful strategy to engage the entire staff is to bring staff development to their classrooms.

You can start a program in which teachers spend an hour of their day visiting multiple classrooms to observe other teachers informally. Staff development meetings can include time to discuss observations from these sessions, and a form can be completed as a means to debrief and process the experience (although it should not be used as a tool for formal evaluation). This is a great way to give teachers firsthand, observational experience with their school climate. This is very effective in engaging the staff at large and personalizing information to enable whole-school reform.

Question: How do we increase credibility of the staff development effort?

Answer: A successful strategy to increase credibility of staff development efforts is to bring in experts.

Bringing in experts can emphasize the fact that those in charge really want to change the current practice. "Money talks" in our society, and when staff see that the administration is spending resources to make changes, that often results in more staff buy-in than if all the work were done by peers. A critical component to outside trainers is continuity and consistency. Almost all staff members respond more favorably to having trainers appear repeatedly, and materials should be available for use on a regular basis for those teachers who end up championing the cause. It is also critical to identify your internal champions and support them, and to solicit their opinion on obstacles and solutions. For schools interested in creating a more asset-building staff, consider the training *Building Developmental Assets in School Communities,* delivered by Search Institute Training and Speaking. For youth-serving organizations, consider the training *More Than Just a Place to Go: Using Developmental Assets to Strengthen Your Youth-Serving Program* or *Infusing Assets into Your Organization,* also delivered by Search Institute Training and Speaking.

Time

"If you value it, you will schedule it." This mantra is understood by staff everywhere. In a school, if the administration wants teachers to work collaboratively, teachers will know the administration is serious when it makes a commitment to creating a time for that work in teachers' schedules, rather than expecting teachers to do it on their own time. Schools are being pressured with trainings in many areas—reading, math, differentiated instruction—and staff members understand that if the administration dedicates time during the day to a training, it truly values that training. If multiple trainings occur in the same area, the importance of the issue is highlighted.

Learning new strategies can be most effective when staff members are able to gather in learning communities that meet regularly to do collective learning, planning, and problem solving. If you are currently using learning communities to address curricular or programmatic areas, you may choose to spend some of the time of these groups on building and deepening asset-building practices. You may also decide that because asset building involves all staff, not just instructional staff, it may be more effective to reconfigure learning communities around the topic of developing strength-based strategies with students, mixing staff from several different groups.

There is no hard-and-fast answer to the best way to group staff members or even the best size of groups for this work, but it is important to carve out regular and recurring time for staff to gather and develop these skills together.

Leadership

To make this effort successful, leaders need to be engaged in the work and attentive to the needs and progress of staff. Leaders in every school or organization are pressed to attend to funding, community relations, content leadership, and many other arenas, but nurturing and building an asset-rich environment with staff who both understand and have the necessary skills to maximize positive youth development does not happen without the care, attention, and support of key leaders. In addition to the important tasks of guaranteeing the time and resources staff need to do this work, a leader also needs to show by example the importance of asset building.

An effective leader needs to model, in his or her own behaviors toward students, the asset-building strategies that staff members are working to develop. These efforts may include but are not limited to:

- Reviewing discipline policies with an eye toward making them strength-based (as an example, posting "Thank you for walking in the halls" signs in place of "No running" signs).

- Reviewing job descriptions and hiring practices to align them. Job descriptions can be written in a way that explicitly states expectations about how students are to be treated, and interviews can be conducted in such a way as to look for asset-rich behavior. For example, candidates applying for jobs in the New Richmond, Wisconsin, school district are given a tour by students. The students then give feedback to the hiring committee as to whether the candidates were "hallway friendly," and their feedback figures into the hiring decision.

- Creating reward and recognition programs to support staff in their efforts to shift behaviors and practices.

- Identifying ways students can be involved in appropriate governance and advisory roles, including ways they can also be working on asset-building skills for themselves and their peers.

Resources

In addition to time for professional development activities, staff members need the resources to support this work, including, for example, trainings, printed materials, and the means to create new materials that allow them to implement creative approaches to asset building in their buildings and in their classrooms. In some cases support might include whatever is necessary for responding to individual young people who are in need of special assistance. We sometimes think of resources primarily in terms of money, but in some instances they might also be knowledge of community help that can be tapped into, or visits or calls with other staffs who have developed their own competencies in this area.

Chapter 2

Building an Asset-Rich Program: Things to Consider

When you dig deeper into the specific assets, you can see that there are some core adult attitudes and behaviors that play a big part in delivering these assets to young people.

Mindset, Assets, and Professional Development

Mindset, discussed in the previous chapter, applies not only to the way people deal with change internally but also to the way people interact with others—and it is especially powerful when it comes to dealing with youth. When staff members hold a growth mindset about themselves, they are open to self-reflection and the idea of improving through thinking about their current practices, learning new strategies, and incorporating them into their work. They are open to this because the growth mindset is an assumption that one can always improve with practice. In contrast, the fixed mindset rests on an assumption that one's ability and talent are innate, and that needing to practice something is actually a sign that one does not have the innate talent or skill. It is critical to recognize the impact of mindset as professional development proceeds with staff.

Every staff will have some members with each of these mindsets. Some staff will hold a growth mindset about themselves but a fixed mindset when it comes to their students' strengths, talents, or abilities. Or, conversely, perhaps they have come to see that their students can improve with practice, but they have not yet examined the fixed nature of their beliefs about themselves and their own ability to change.

When mindset is explored in conjunction with professional development and the topic is Developmental Assets, phenomenal results can occur. Research has shown that staff expectations of their students have a powerful impact on the achievement of those students.[1] When staff members hold the mindset that their students can achieve through well-executed lessons and time for practice, students rise to meet these expectations. An entire category of the Developmental Assets is devoted to this idea—the Boundaries and Expectations category.

It is important for staff to hold this same growth mindset of themselves, since modeling behavior has been shown to be one of the key ways young people learn something. It is powerful to share personal stories with students in teaching Asset 32: Planning and Decision Making. When teachers or staff persons tell students they can set goals, learn new material, and achieve results through their own efforts, *and* can demonstrate that they, as adults, do this themselves, it is a powerful way to reinforce the message.

The delivery of many of the Developmental Assets depends on this growth mindset. A staff person will not be effective in helping a young person develop, for example, Asset 29: Honesty, or Asset 32: Planning and Decision Making, if that staff member believes a person is either born honest and organized or is not. Only when staff see that these traits and skills can be developed through the formal lessons they deliver and the informal interactions they have with students can they be effective in building these assets with and for students.

The concept of mindset and change gets at complex beliefs that staff have acquired over a lifetime, and changing those beliefs takes formal attention, practice, and structured opportunities for reflection, but can pay off in the impact higher expectations of all students can yield.

Building Healthy Relationships

Few staff people would say that they have a hard time building relationships with students. They might tell you that they believe it is important to maintain a professional distance from students (and on a number of dimensions, they are absolutely right). They might say that some students make it difficult if not impossible to form relationships with them (and we know that this can also be true). But many staff members have not had formal training in how to build relationships with students. They've been told what *not* to do in interactions with students, but not how to consciously strengthen their connections with youth. The assets are based on building healthy relationships, and there are skills that will improve these relationships in ways that help both staff and students thrive.

---

1. H.M. Cooper, "A Historical Overview of Teacher Expectation Effects" (paper presented at the Annual Convention of the American Psychological Association, 91st, Anaheim, CA, August 1983).

Chapter 4 has several activities that allow staff to develop a list of behaviors related to relationships that can serve as a guide to practice. Even given the restrictions on student-staff interactions (which have been set in an effort to protect both the student and the staff person), there are ways to create the personal interactions that young people need in order to feel safe, to feel heard, and to feel that they matter.

Making Asset Building Intentional

One of the biggest roadblocks to making asset building a part of a professional development plan or program is that most adults who work with young people already feel they have the skills they need to build assets, or have not given the skills involved much thought.

Reflect on the kind of training most staff have received, in college or on the job, which specifically equips them to understand the strengths young people need to thrive and helps them refine the skills that prepare them to form caring, supportive relationships with the young people with whom they work. Some staff members are "naturals." They seem able to connect with a wide range of students. Some staff members have received basic training in how to work in strength-based ways with young people. And most would tell you that they chose their job because they care about the development of young people and want to contribute to their success. But all too many have not received the initial training or the ongoing support to build upon the natural instincts they bring to the job.

Because working with young people seems like common sense, and something that "comes naturally" to people who have chosen to work with youth, it can be a challenge to view this complex set of behaviors through a critical lens. But common sense is not necessarily common practice.

For example, the framework of Developmental Assets is intentionally worded in language that seems like "common sense." Very few of the 40 assets would strike an adult as an illogical or difficult thing to provide for youth. It is only when adults reflect on the specific actions that were carried out by asset builders in their own lives and then start to name and describe in detail where their own opportunities for deeper asset building lie, as well as what strategies they might employ to forge more supportive relationships with youth, that they realize the depths there are to be plumbed. A second challenge surrounding this idea is that adults often believe they are already building assets, but a study of adult beliefs about what young people need and their actual behaviors points to a gap that needs to be addressed.

In a study of adult social norms, conducted by Search Institute in 2000 and again in 2002 in concert with the Gallup Organization, several key findings emerged.

Three-fourths of a national random sample of adults agreed that 19 actions based on specific Developmental Assets were important for adults to provide to young people, with 8 of those items being identified as most important by 70 percent or more of the adults surveyed.

The top-ranked actions were:

- Encourage success in school   90%
- Expect parents to set boundaries   84%
- Teach shared values   80%
- Teach respect for cultural differences   77%
- Guide decision making   76%
- Give financial guidance   75%
- Have meaningful conversations   75%
- Discuss personal values   73%[2]

These high rankings held true across different levels of education and income and across various ethnic groups, pointing to a true consensus by adults on what young people need from the adults in our society.

But when researchers followed up with the questions "How many of the adults you know actually do this? Would you say almost all, a large majority, half, some, or very few?" they were able to point out the gap that exists between what actions adults believe are important and their actual engagement in these actions.

The following chart displays those top items, now placed in order of the size of the gap between perceived importance and engagement:[3]

	IMPORTANCE	ENGAGEMENT	GAP
Expect parents to set boundaries	84%	42%	42%
Teach respect for cultural differences	77	36	41
Have meaningful conversations	75	34	41
Give financial guidance	75	36	39
Discuss personal values	73	37	36
Teach shared values	80	45	35
Guide decision making	76	41	35
Encourage success in school	90	69	21

2. Peter C. Scales, *Other People's Kids: Social Expectations and American Adults' Involvement with Children and Adolescents* (New York: Kluwer Academic/Plenum, 2003), 101.
3. Ibid., 105.

These striking results remind us that even though there may be consensus on positive adult actions, too few adults are acting on these beliefs.

Young people note this absence of adults in their lives, as well. In the 2003 data set, which surveyed more than 148,000 students in grades 6–12 using Search Institute's *Profiles of Student Life: Attitudes and Behaviors* survey, only 43 percent said that they received support from three or more nonparent adults. So, while the Developmental Assets seem like common sense, adults can fall short of making them common practice.

It's important to bridge the gap between *acknowledgment* and *action*. The activities and exercises that follow are designed to help you do just that.

STAFF DEVELOPMENT PRACTICE

Chapter 3

A PowerPoint Presentation Introducing the Developmental Assets

This script can be used as the basis for an introductory presentation on the Developmental Assets. The accompanying PowerPoint presentation can be found on the CD-ROM that came with this book. Feel free to personalize this script as you read it aloud, improvising based on your needs and the needs of your school or youth program.

In addition to the PowerPoint presentation, you'll need enough copies of the list of 40 Developmental Assets (found on the CD-ROM) for every attendee. You'll give the list to them before the presentation starts.

If you would like to receive further training on how to present information about the assets to a wide range of audiences, consider the *Everyone's an Asset Builder* training or the *Training of Trainers: Essentials of Asset Building* available through Search Institute Training and Speaking (www.search-institute.org/training-speaking).

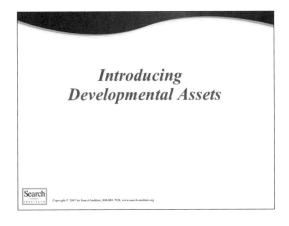

Slide 1. Introducing Developmental Assets

Hello and thank you for joining us for today's presentation, *Introducing Developmental Assets*.

I'm [your name] and [something about yourself, including why you are interested in sharing information about the Developmental Assets].

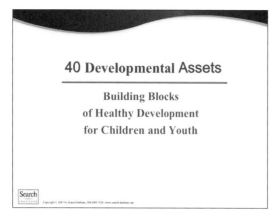

Slide 2. 40 Developmental Assets—Building Blocks of Healthy Development

I'd like to take you back to your own teenage years. Now . . . think about an adult who made a positive difference in your life. Who was it? And what did that person do? Hold that memory, because we'll be going back to it a little later.

I'd like to start with a little background about Search Institute, the organization that created the Developmental Assets framework. They are a national not-for-profit organization and have been conducting research about young people for over 50 years. In the late '70s and early '80s they were involved, as were many other groups, in identifying and understanding how risky behaviors could derail young people as they moved toward adulthood. Researchers there saw that many programs designed to minimize these risky behaviors had a positive effect, but that effect weakened as young people went back into the community that had raised them.

Peter Benson, president of Search Institute, felt there had to be a different way of looking at this puzzle. He wondered, "If it takes a village to raise a child, what does it take to raise a village?"

He also noticed that while researchers were getting better at naming all the effects of various risky behaviors, and why young people shouldn't engage in them, there wasn't much conversation about what positive actions young people could take or positive supports adults could supply to young people to help them thrive.

After reexamining the research on young people, and convening groups of practitioners, Search Institute scientists identified some basic **building blocks of healthy development** that both research and common sense affirmed as leading to positive outcomes.

Slide 3. Icons for Eight Asset Categories

You should have in front of you the **handout listing the 40 Developmental Assets.** That looks like a lot, but we're going to dive right in and make that list more manageable.

The first thing you will notice is that the list is divided in half.

The first 20 assets are what we refer to as the **External Assets.** As you glance down the list you will notice that these are external structures, relationships, and activities that create a positive environment for young people.

The last 20 assets we refer to as **Internal Assets.** These are internal values, skills, and beliefs that young people also need to fully engage with and function in the world around them.

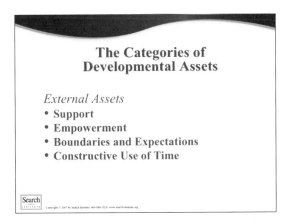

Slide 4. The Categories of Developmental Assets— External Assets

Now let's go a little deeper. Twenty is still a big list, but you can see that the 20 external assets are subdivided into four categories.

The first is **Support.** Young people need to be surrounded by people who love, care for, appreciate, and accept them. The assets in this category name how and where young people experience support.

The second is **Empowerment.** Young people need to feel valued and valuable. They also need to feel safe.

The third is **Boundaries and Expectations.** Young people need clear rules and consistent consequences. They also need encouragement to do their best.

The fourth is **Constructive Use of Time.** Young people need opportunities outside of school to learn and develop new skills and interests with other youth and adults.

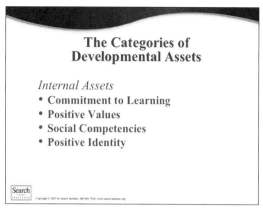

The Categories of
Developmental Assets

Internal Assets
• Commitment to Learning
• Positive Values
• Social Competencies
• Positive Identity

Slide 5. The Categories of Developmental Assets— Internal Assets

The internal assets are also subdivided into four categories.

The first is **Commitment to Learning.** Young people need a sense of the lasting importance of learning and a belief in their own abilities.

The second is **Positive Values.** Young people need to develop strong guiding values to help them make healthy choices.

The third is **Social Competencies.** Young people need the skills to interact effectively with others and cope with new situations.

The fourth is **Positive Identity.** Young people need to believe in their own self-worth and to feel they have control over things that happen to them.

Remember back to that adult you identified as being important to you when you were a teenager. That person was building assets in you, even if she or he didn't know it or call it that. You can do that for the young people in your life.

Before the next slide . . .

In order to measure the presence or absence of these Developmental Assets in the lives of young people, researchers at Search Institute designed a survey for students in grades 6 through 12. It asks questions that funnel into each of the assets, and also asks about whether young people have engaged in any of 24 risk-taking behaviors and 8 thriving behaviors as well.

At that point, I think they asked a very interesting question. Instead of asking which of these building blocks or Developmental Assets was the most important, they instead asked: Does the number of Developmental Assets a young person experiences make a difference?

And here is what they found:

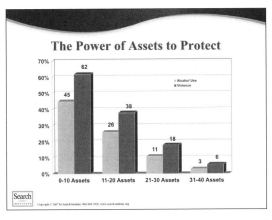

Slide 6. The Power of Assets to Protect

We'll look at just two of the risky behaviors: Alcohol Use and Violence.

On the left side of the chart are those youth who **experienced the fewest assets in their lives: 0 to 10 of them. Forty-five percent of that group** had used alcohol in the last 30 days and/or had been drunk in the last two weeks. When we jump to the right side of the chart, we see that in the group of students who experience 31 to 40 assets in their lives, just 3 percent were drinking.

The same pattern applies when we look at **violence,** although the numbers change. **Sixty-two percent of those students with the fewest assets** are using physical violence, threatening violence, or carrying weapons, compared to just **6 percent of those students with the most assets.**

This pattern runs across the 24 risk-taking behaviors Search Institute has studied, that is, the more assets a young person experiences, the fewer risk-taking behaviors he or she is likely to engage in.

And what connections did Search Institute find to the **thriving behaviors**?

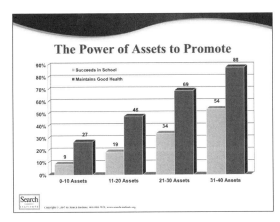

Slide 7. The Power of Assets to Promote

The more assets a young person experiences, the more likely he or she is to also report engaging in some of the eight thriving behaviors. This chart shows us two of them: Succeeding in School (which is measured by asking if students received mostly As) and Maintaining Good Health (which is measured by questions about nutrition and exercise.) And the fewer assets they experience, the fewer thriving behaviors they engage in.

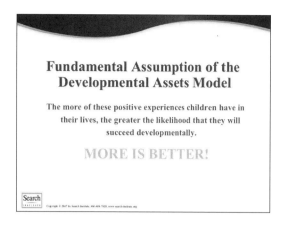

Slide 8. Fundamental Assumption of the Developmental Assets Model

One fundamental assumption of the Developmental Assets model is that the more of these positive experiences young people have in their lives, the greater the likelihood that they will succeed developmentally. More is better.

TIME CHECK—MIDPOINT

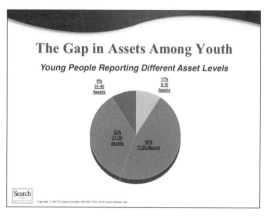

Slide 9. The Gap in Assets Among Youth—Pie Chart

If most of our young people experienced 31 to 40 of the assets, we could be confident that we were doing all we could to equip young people with the strengths and supports they need to thrive.

Unfortunately, just 8 percent of the young people surveyed by Search Institute are that well equipped by the adults around them. Another 32 percent experience 21 to 30 assets—heading in the right direction.

But that leaves over **half of our young people experiencing fewer than half** of the developmental building blocks they need for optimum development, with 17 percent experiencing 10 or fewer assets in their lives.

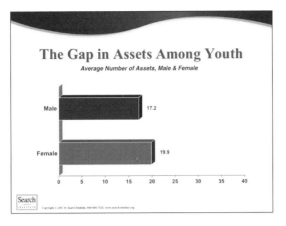

Slide 10. The Gap in Assets among Youth—Boys and Girls

On average, girls experience slightly more assets than do boys.

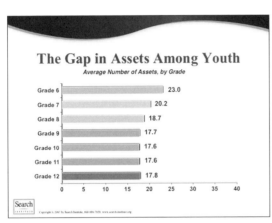

Slide 11. The Gap in Assets among Youth—by Grade

The average number of assets experienced by young people starts to drop from grade 6 through grade 11, with a slight rebound beginning in grade 12.

I'm sure you could name some of the reasons this might be happening: the impact of puberty, the change from the self-contained classrooms of the elementary years to the multiple teachers and classrooms youth have to navigate as they move into middle school and high school, the number of school changes they experience, and the growing influence of their peers. Some of you might even suggest that as young people enter their teens, adults assume teens need them less and inadvertently pull away from young people—but the truth is that teens do need caring adults in their lives, even through they don't always know how to ask us for our support.

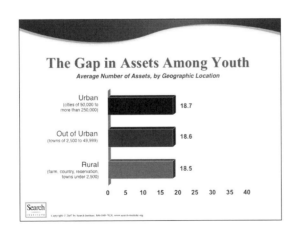

Slide 12. The Gap in Assets among Youth—by Geographic Location

Many adults see this information about the Developmental Assets and assume that location will make a big difference.

The reality is that we see little difference in the average number of assets youth report based on where they live.

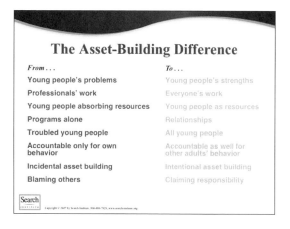

Slide 13. The Asset-Building Difference

What does it look like when adults pay attention to this information and try to put asset building into practice? We begin to see some fundamental shifts in the ways adults think and act:

From:	*To:*
A focus on young people's problems	Seeing young people's strengths
Seeing the raising of young people as the work of professionals	Seeing raising young people as everyone's work
Viewing youth as absorbing resources	Viewing youth as resources
Assuming programs alone can raise young people	Understanding that all adults contribute to the relationships that are fundamental to healthy youth
A primary focus on troubled youth	A wider focus on all youth
An assumption that we are responsible only for our own behaviors	An understanding that we are also accountable for other adults' behaviors
A complacency that incidental asset building is enough	A new effort to be intentional in our asset-building efforts
Blaming others ("those parents, those teachers")	Claiming our responsibility for the health of young people in our community

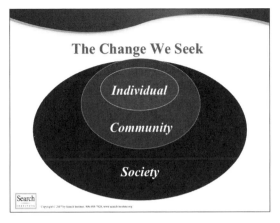

Slide 14. The Change We Seek

We want all individuals to understand these fundamental building blocks that help our young people grow up to be responsible, caring, and productive adults.

We want those individuals to engage their communities in paying closer attention to the young people in their midst and providing them with the fundamental building blocks they need.

We can all work toward the societal shifts that can help young people feel affirmed and welcomed instead of blamed and marginalized.

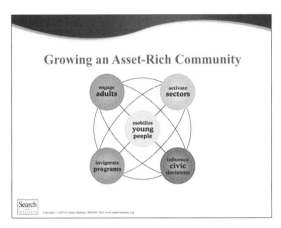

Slide 15. Growing an Asset-Rich Community

Five action strategies can help community initiatives grow this new way of thinking and acting on behalf of young people.

Engage Adults from all walks of life so they can build relationships with young people.

Activate Sectors so that businesses and congregations and schools and government all see their stake in raising healthy youth and the roles they can play.

Mobilize Youth to be a part of the process. Remember that youth can be powerful asset builders for themselves, for their peers, and for younger children. And that being part of local asset-building efforts builds assets in those youth at the same time they are building assets in others.

Invigorate Programs. The asset framework doesn't require a new curriculum. It invites program providers to focus on the environment they create for young people and the relationships they build with them. As providers think more intentionally about the places where their programs can build assets, those programs will become stronger.

Finally, **Influence Civic Decision Makers** who make policies and create funding streams that affect youth and who also shape public opinion.

More than 600 communities are already focusing on creating healthier, more attentive places for their young people to grow up. And thousands of individuals are trying to be more intentional as they connect with young people in their communities.

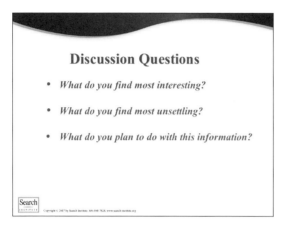

Slide 16. Discussion Questions

Our time is almost up, but I invite you to think about the questions on this slide. Turn to the person sitting next to you and tell him or her which question is most interesting to you, and why.

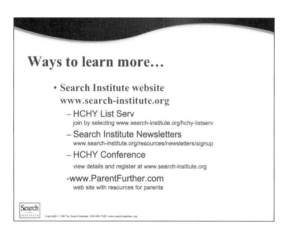

Slide 17. Ways to Learn More

Search Institute has developed trainings, books, posters, and other materials to help asset builders learn and share.

If you would like to join the Healthy Communities • Healthy Youth listserv, the link is on this slide. You can also sign up there to receive periodic e-mails from Search Institute.

Chapter 4

Staff Meeting Activities

This chapter includes activities designed for staff meetings—some for large-group gatherings and others for small professional learning communities, or PLCs. That doesn't mean, however, that these activities are strictly one or the other; you'll find that some large-scale activities can be easily adapted to fit PLCs and vice versa.

This collection of activities is also designed to deepen staff understanding of assets and give them a stronger sense of how the Developmental Assets play out in their lives. Inventories, peer discussion, and reflection activities all combine to highlight the role assets have in everything we do, both personally and when we are working with youth.

Rare Birds

Objective

To help the staff connect with one another and build community.

This activity is completed at a staff meeting early in the year, and information is shared at meetings all year long. This exercise can also be completed by teachers with their classes to build a more connected community.

Time Required

10 minutes at the first staff meeting; 2 minutes at subsequent meetings

Materials Needed

Rare Birds handout (one per participant)

Instructions

Ask staff to fill out the following form during a staff meeting and turn it in. Then, at meetings throughout the year, draw a slip from the collection and read it aloud. Ask staff to guess who this "Rare Bird" is; provide hints as necessary.

Rare Birds

Name:

From the following categories, select one in which you feel you are unique (you may choose more than one category). Write down specifically what makes you unique in that category. Put your name on the paper, fold it, and turn it in to the facilitator without anyone seeing what you wrote.

Throughout the year the facilitator will draw a slip from this collection and read it to the staff and ask them to guess who this "rare bird" might be.

Surprising facts:

Interesting job:

Favorite food:

Interesting experience:

Special awards:

Special skills:

Special interests:

Building Connections

Objective

To help the staff connect with one another and build community.

This activity provides an opportunity for staff to connect with one another and learn about commonalities and differences they share. This exercise can also be completed by teachers with their classes to help build a more connected classroom.

Time Required

30 minutes

Materials Needed

8½" x 11" piece of paper for each participant

Instructions

Have participants divide their papers into six equal sections and label each section with a letter (A through F). Then have them write or draw a picture to answer to the following questions in the corresponding section:

A. What was your favorite toy as a child?

B. If you could go to any concert, what concert would you attend? Whom would you invite to go with you?

C. What is your favorite memory as a child?

D. Who were two teachers you are glad you had?

E. What is your favorite comfort food?

F. Draw a picture of yourself in retirement.

After staff have answered the questions, one in each lettered section, have each of the participants choose a partner he or she doesn't know very well. Ask one person in each pair to share one or two answers to the questions with his or her partner. After three minutes, alternate who is speaking in the pair. If time allows, have participants switch partners and share their answers with a new person.

Self-Care Bingo

Objective

To help the staff be aware of stress and create and share skills to relieve stress.

Everyone has stress, so this is a good way to get people talking about it—and sharing ways to beat it. This information can be used throughout the year to assist colleagues in managing their stress and building a caring community.

Time Required

30 minutes

Materials Needed

What I Do to Relieve Stress handout (one per participant)

Instructions

Explain the following categories of stress relievers: immediate coping skills, daily supportive activities, pleasurable joys, physical nourishment, emotional well-being, social connection, and lifelong foundations.

Immediate coping skills are quick and effective ways to restore a sense of balance. They are very useful in day-to-day experiences, *but alone they are not enough*. They include deep breathing, muscle relaxation, visualization, self-talk, and taking a break.

Daily supportive activities include pleasurable joys, physical nourishment, emotional well-being, and social connection—activities that support immediate coping skills.

Pleasurable joys include soothing scents, music, touch, humor, warmth, and play.

Physical nourishment includes rest, healthy eating, and physical activity.

Emotional well-being is nurturing a sense of optimism and self-esteem, and expressing feelings.

Social connection involves volunteering, caring for others, performing kind deeds, and building healthy relationships.

Lifelong foundations are the life balancers that often can give you a sense of harmony. They provide meaning in what you are doing: meditation/prayer, connection with nature, viewing challenges as opportunities, connection with a higher power, and reflection on values and goals.

Now distribute the What I Do to Relieve Stress sheets and ask participants to fill in seven of the nine empty squares with things they do to relieve stress.

When participants have completed the sheets, have them move around the room, find other people who have listed similar ways to relieve stress, and sign each other's squares. Each person may sign another person's sheet only once. The two extra squares should be completed with new activities participants learned while they were looking at others' self-care exercise sheets.

What I Do to Relieve Stress

School Roster Stars

Objective

To help the staff identify students who are connected to school staff and those who need stronger connections.

Time Required

30 minutes

Materials Needed

A school roster printed in 24-point or larger type, triple spaced, one name per line
A colored marker or five stickers for each staff member

Instructions

Print out a full school roster. It should be triple spaced, in a large font (24-point or larger) with only one name per line. Tape all pages of the roster to the walls of the room where the staff meeting is being held.

Give staff members a colored marker or five stickers each, and instruct them to mark a star or place their stickers next to the names of five students that they feel they have a relationship with (i.e., they know more about the students than just their performance in their own classes). After all staff have completed marking or placing their stickers on the roster, have a discussion regarding the students who have either few or no stars or stickers by their names. Share strategies about who is going to try to connect with these currently unconnected students. This activity can be surprising: staff who have done this activity have noted that certain students often have several stars or stickers, while many other students have none.

The School Roster Stars activity can be done several times a year. Staff can celebrate the increased number of students with stars by their names and redouble their efforts with students who have received few or no stars.

Student Challenges

Objective

To share strategies for dealing with student behaviors.

One common issue for school staff is dealing with challenging student behaviors. An effective but often overlooked strategy is to solve problems as a team or group. This activity works in a large-group setting or in a small professional learning community.

Time Required

30 minutes

Materials Needed

A note card for each participant

Instructions

Distribute note cards and ask everyone to write down one student issue he or she is currently struggling with (e.g., student failure, difficulty connecting with guardians, students in hallways without passes, dress-code violations). Staff should not sign their cards, but rather return them to the facilitator anonymously. The facilitator should briefly read all cards and select one to three issues that seem to be a theme for the staff.

To begin the meeting, ask people to arrange themselves in teams of four to six members and assign each group one theme or problem. Allow each team 15 minutes to brainstorm positive solutions to its issue. Then have each small group share its solutions with the large group (the facilitator should record all ideas). This process will provide solutions to the staff members, allow multiple perspectives from a variety of individuals, challenge their current approaches in a positive manner, and provide staff a mechanism to see their own strengths and resources.

Staff Awards

Objective
To help the staff and students connect.

In this activity, students vote for staff in various award categories. It's a great way to get the entire school involved.

Time Required
Varies

Materials Needed
Ballots and ballot box

Instructions
Draft a ballot that lists categories such as:

The staff member most likely to be (or to have been) in a rock band

The staff member with the most organized desk

The staff member most likely to travel the farthest during the year

The staff member with the most welcoming room

The staff member with the kindest smile

The staff member with the oddest jokes

. . . and so on. Explain that all staff are eligible for the awards, and ask students to drop their ballots in a box in the lunchroom (enlist the student council or other student leadership group to distribute ballots and count votes).

Name the winners for each category at a staff meeting and present them with appropriate gag gifts if you wish. Then highlight the winners during school announcements or showcase them in the school newspaper.

All the World's a Stage

Objective

To use the arts to see and present asset-building actions.

Sometimes it's hard to envision exactly how an asset-building interaction might look. This activity is designed to make staff think about what they should be looking for when they see asset building in action.

Time Required

30–60 minutes depending on the number of staff members

Materials Needed

None, though theater props can make the activity more entertaining

Instructions

Divide staff into teams of two or three to plan, script, and act out one of the Developmental Assets. Set a two- to three-minute time limit for each presentation. A variation on this activity is to ask staff to script a non-asset-building moment, act it out, and invite any other team to come up and reenact the situation in a more asset-rich way.

Asset Building Is Like/Not Like

Objective

To get staff using metaphors and objects to expand their thinking about Developmental Assets.

When we work with students, we are constantly thinking about new ways to present information so that it "sticks." Use these activities in staff meetings to expand staff members' thinking about assets and help them retain it for easy access when necessary.

Time Required

Variable: tailor this activity to take more or less time depending on your needs

Materials Needed

A random assortment of materials such as rubber bands, rulers, flashlights, coins, other small items

Instructions

Remind staff that just as they use a variety of prompts to get their students' minds going, so they can do the same for themselves. Divide staff into groups of three to five people and give them an item. You can give each group the same item, or distribute different items to different groups. Ask each group to think about and discuss how asset building or the asset framework is like their item. (For example, a rubber band is like asset building because stretching a rubber band is hard at first but gets easier the more you stretch it, just as asset building feels a little stiff when you start trying to be intentional about it and gets easier with practice.)

Depending on the time available, you can limit conversations to the groups, or ask them to report to the entire staff. If you have time, repeat the exercise, this time asking groups to name how the item is *not* like asset building.

A variation on this activity is to assign each group an animal and ask participants to think about how that animal relates to asset building. (A barnacle bonds to a surface, just as we want a student to bond to school; dolphins have been shown to exhibit caring behavior, just as we want students to show caring toward others.)

I Noticed!

Objective

To keep asset-building activities at the forefront of the staff's awareness.

It's important for staff members to be aware of how assets are put into practice, and this exercise is an effective means to accomplish this goal.

Time Required

A few minutes a day for a week

Materials Needed

Search Institute's "I Noticed!" notes or small cards that read "Caught you building assets" (at least three for each participant)

Instructions

Use Search Institute's "I Noticed!" notes or photocopy some business-size cards with the message "Caught you building assets." At a staff meeting, hand out several of them to each staff member and say that the goal is to spot someone building assets and give him or her one of the cards. On the back, staff members should sign their names and note briefly what the person was doing to build assets. The object of the "game" is to get rid of all the cards they started with. You can also make this an ongoing activity by distributing new cards at every staff meeting.

Observe and Report

Objective

To help staff identify areas where asset building happens in your school.

Sometimes building assets has everything to do with a time or place. Use this activity to help you identify the areas in your school where asset building happens most, and then use the results to help staff focus on and improve other spaces.

Time Required

A few minutes a day for a week

Materials Needed

Observe and Report handout (one per participant)

Instructions

At a staff meeting, assign staff members specific areas in the school or youth center that they are to watch during the coming week (depending on the size of your building or the number of staff, you can assign several people to each space). Give them the Observe and Report handout and tell them their task for the next week is to spot asset building going on in that space and describe it at the next staff meeting. What asset building is observed after school in the lounge? What asset building takes place at the front desk? In the lunchroom? The computer lab? The classrooms? Don't forget to include the staff areas as well.

Observe and Report

Staff member's name:

Space I observed:

Times I observed this space:

Things about this space that indicated it was welcoming to students
(and parents and staff):

Easy things that could make this space more welcoming:

Positive/asset-building behaviors I saw taking place in this space:

Negative/non-asset-building behaviors I saw taking place in this space:

My recommendations for making this space more asset rich:

Group Treasure Hunt

Objective

To help build staff connections.

School and youth program staff can sometimes "clump together" based on specialties and job descriptions. This activity is a good way to break up those clumps and help people connect across departments. You can change or add questions and give prizes at the end for teams with the most points or most unusual answers. This exercise can also be used in classrooms and with youth groups.

Time Required

30 minutes

Materials Needed

Group Treasure Hunt handout (one per team)

Instructions

At a staff meeting, assign staff who typically don't work or socialize together into teams of five. Give each team a Group Treasure Hunt handout and ask teams to nominate a recorder within each group; the recorder will keep a tally of the points her or his team "earns" for each question. Explain that the purpose of this activity is to learn about the unique aspects of their coworkers and just have fun in a group. After questions are answered and scores are totaled, have the teams share in the large group.

Group Treasure Hunt

Give **one point**:

- for each person living in team members' homes.

- for each button on each team member's clothes.

- for each team member who was born outside the state.

- for each pet in team members' families (multiple fish count as one pet).

- for each shoelace hole or hook on one shoe of each team member.

- for each team member who has lived in a state other than this one.

- for each team member who has flown overseas.

- for each musical instrument team members know how to play.

- for each organized sports team on which team members have participated in the past year.

- for each member with brown hair,
  two for each with blond,
  three for each with black,
  four for each with red,
  and **five** for each with a color not listed here.

Remember and Repeat

Objective

To help staff understand the impact of asset building.

Sometimes asset building can seem abstract and theoretical. This activity, adapted from the PowerPoint presentation in Chapter 3, helps staff members connect to asset building in a personal way. They can also use this activity in meetings with parents to help them understand the impact asset building had on their lives.

Time Required

20–30 minutes

Materials Needed

None

Instructions

Have staff members think about their favorite teacher during their teenage years. Ask them to remember that teacher's classroom: "What did it look like? Smell like? Who was in class with you? What did you look like? What did you like about this teacher?" Tell them to take a minute and reconstruct what they liked about this individual and the environment they were in.

After one minute, ask all staff to get a partner and spend three minutes each describing her or his favorite teacher.

Then bring the conversation back to the large group and ask staff to share details about their favorite teachers. Responses often include having a sense of humor, knowing about and supporting aspects of life outside of school, and making learning fun.

Next have the group look for similarities in the responses. Typically there will be very few, if any, responses that are subject specific (e.g., "She was my favorite teacher because I loved geometry"). Loving the teacher rarely has anything to do with that teacher's subject, although many may have pursued studies in that subject area because of a teacher's impact.

Tell the staff: "Those teachers were building assets in you, even if they didn't know it or call it that. Remember the importance asset building had on you as a child and recognize that you can do the same thing for the young people in your life."

Values Sort

Objective

To help staff identify and discuss personal values and connect them with Developmental Assets.

Developmental Assets are closely connected to personal values. Use this exercise to identify and discuss the personal values that each staff member holds. Feel free to add to the list other values, such as morality, creativity, emotional well-being, love, knowledge, honesty, wealth, health, achievement, loyalty, power, autonomy, altruism, recognition, wisdom, or justice. You can also use this exercise to facilitate discussion with youth.

Time Required

30 minutes

Materials Needed

Values Sort handout (one per participant)

Instructions

Distribute the Values Sort handout to each individual. Ask the staff to sit in groups of four to six, but have each staff member complete the activity independently. After everyone has finished, have the small groups use the discussion questions to facilitate conversation.

Values Sort

Directions: There are 12 values listed on the reverse of this page. Examine the values and place them in order of importance to you from 1 to 12. After the group is finished, use the following questions as a guide for a discussion.

1. Identify your top six values and explain why they are important to you.

2. Identify your bottom six values and explain why they are not as important to you.

3. Discuss whether this time in your life has changed the ranking of your values.

4. Have you ever felt that your values were compromised and if so, why?

5. If you had to take away the bottom two values on your list, what would that change for you?

6. Are there any values currently not listed that you would trade for ones on the list?

Values Sort

Belonging
To feel a strong sense of mutual connection with family, friends, your work, etc.

Control
To feel a sense of personal power in your own life

Creativity
To have opportunities in your work and/or personal life to create new and original ideas, concepts, programs, etc.

Growth/Learning
To have ongoing opportunities for personal growth and development

Health/Wellness
To be actively involved in maintaining and enhancing your overall well-being

Independence
To have freedom of thought and action in your personal and work life

Leisure/Lifestyle
To structure your life in a way that affords you enough leisure time and/or your preferred lifestyle

Pleasure
To enjoy life

Principles
To live in harmony with a personally meaningful ethical code or set of principles

Risk/Security
To maintain acceptable levels of risk-taking and stability-seeking issues in your life

Service
To contribute to the betterment of the lives of others

Spirituality
To be connected with an integrating positive force in the universe
(God, higher power, consciousness, nature, etc.)

Community Support

Objective

To help staff identify and connect with community resources.

Schools and youth programs don't exist in a vacuum: they are integral parts of a larger community. And just as communities rely on you to nurture and teach their children, you should turn to the resources in your community for support. This exercise helps staff pool their knowledge to identify the areas where the greater community can lend its help.

Time Required

15–30 minutes

Materials Needed

Community Support handout (one per participant)

Instructions

During a staff meeting, ask individual staff members to complete the Community Support handout. Have staff first share their reflections in small groups, and then share the common ideas they discovered with the large group. Record all the community resources that the staff listed, and have a discussion about how these agencies can be more integrally connected to the ongoing work of the school community. At the conclusion of the meeting, decide who will be responsible for connecting with community resources and outline the next steps. Individual staff members can keep their Community Support handouts.

Community Support

With the current challenges the school is facing,

I want . . .

I can . . .

I dislike . . .

I am . . .

I need . . .

I will try . . .

Current community resources that are helping or could help are . . .

Seeing Is Believing

Objective

To give staff practice in observing and describing asset-building actions in detail.

Staff frequently believe they "know asset building when they see it." This activity helps them develop their abilities to describe what they are seeing and identify the concrete actions that make up an asset-building act. If you are focusing on a specific asset category for a given time period (a week or a month), then tie this activity to that asset category, revisiting this activity each time you shift categories.

Time Required

A few minutes a day for a week, then 10–20 minutes at the next staff meeting to discuss results

Materials Needed

Observing Assets in Action handout (three per participant)

Instructions

Announce at a staff meeting that for the following week, you want staff to look for adults at your school or youth center who are acting on one of the eight asset categories. Give three copies of the Observing Assets in Action handout to each staff member and ask each to record what he or she sees. Post the asset category name in several high-traffic spots to help staff remember the category during they time frame they are to observe it.

Although staff will be observing as individuals, you can have them work in teams of two or three at the next staff meeting to pool their ideas. The winning team (the one with the longest list) can be awarded a prize or recognition of your choosing (certificate, asset category sticker, food, etc.). At each staff meeting, or each time the category that you are focused on changes, assign a new asset category. At the end of the series, ask which category was easiest to see examples of and which category was most difficult. What could people do as a staff to increase their asset-building efforts in the category that was most difficult? Celebrate their efforts and identify the category they feel most confident in building.

Observing Assets in Action

Your name:

The asset category you are observing:

Situation you observed (describe what happened):

Which specific assets did you see being worked on?

What specific actions told you this was asset building in action?

Catch Them in Action

Objective

To help staff see that students can be asset builders, too.

One key component of asset building is to empower students to build assets for themselves, and also with and for others. It is important for staff to learn to identify actions students take to build various assets, reinforcing that youth themselves can be powerful asset builders.

Time Required

A few minutes each day for a week, then 15 minutes to discuss the results at the next staff meeting

Materials Needed

Observing Students Building Assets handout (three per participant)

Instructions

Select several asset categories or choose specific assets. Ask staff to observe and record over the coming week any examples of students building those assets for themselves or their peers. For example, they might include times when students help reinforce classroom rules (Boundaries and Expectations) or they might notice a student giving an honest response, even when it might be easier to bend the truth a little (Asset 29), or following through on the planning and decision making required for a particular project (Asset 32), and so on. Take 15 minutes at the next staff meeting to discuss what you saw and learned.

Observing Students Building Assets

Your name:

The asset or asset category you are observing:

Situation you observed (describe what happened):

Which specific assets did you see being worked on?

What specific actions told you this was asset building in action?

Worth a Thousand Words

Objective

To provide staff with another way of seeing asset building in action.

We often get used to places or actions we see every day, and after a while we cease to notice them. Taking a picture can inspire us, or move us to think differently about those things. Use this activity to bring visual learning into the mix as a tool. (Note: Be sure to check whether your school or program has rules about privacy, photography, or the use of cell phone cameras.)

Time Required

A few minutes each day for a week, then 30 minutes at the next staff meeting to discuss the photos

Materials Needed

A camera for each staff member. Depending on your school's or program's resources, you could buy inexpensive disposable cameras, or ask staff to bring their own cameras from home or use the cameras on their cell phones; you could also "assign" this activity to just a few staff members at a time and ask them to share cameras among themselves.

Instructions

Ask staff to capture one or two asset-building moments over the course of the week. Have the staff e-mail or provide you with the photos before the next staff meeting. At that next staff meeting, display the shots either on paper or by uploading them to a PowerPoint program and projecting them. Ask the photographers to explain what they were trying to capture with the shot. (As a bonus, and after receiving permission from parents and guardians, you could use some of the best shots in newsletters and other public relations materials, or post them during parent/guardian nights.)

Chapter 5

Ongoing Activities

This chapter contains staff development materials designed for long-term use over an entire school year. Seeing messages, information, and reminders in multiple places over time will help staff keep asset-building actions "top of mind." Chapter 5 also includes printed summaries organized by each of the eight Developmental Asset categories. These can be downloaded from the CD-ROM and then printed and distributed through staff boxes or at staff meetings, or sent to staff by e-mail at regular intervals. You'll also find on the CD-ROM several wallet cards to provide daily reminders to staff about the assets they are trying to build and 11 x 17-inch posters that you can hang in staff or public areas to keep assets front and center in staff awareness.

Appreciation Letters

Objective

To help staff support each other.

An easy and effective way to increase staff support is to have staff members write each other letters describing what they notice, admire, or appreciate about their colleagues' work. You can start this activity at the beginning of the year and watch it spread as time goes on.

Time Required

5–10 minutes

Materials Needed

Appreciation Letter handout

Instructions

Make a two-sided copy of the Appreciation Letter handout (so that the same text appears on both sides). Choose five staff members to complete Appreciation Letters, which they can sign or leave anonymous and then deliver to the mailboxes of the people they observed. Each staff person should personalize the note with details on why he or she is choosing to recognize a particular colleague. The recipient will follow the instructions on the letter, which requests that the recipient copy the form and send a letter within seven days to someone he or she has noticed. Soon a large number of the staff will have received peer recognition. Continue this process throughout the year until every staff member has received a letter.

Appreciation Letter

To:

I noticed and appreciate the work you are doing.

This handout is designed to work like a chain letter. Please make a two-sided copy of the uncompleted side of this handout so that the same text appears on both sides of the new copy). Then fill out one side and send it to a colleague within seven days.

Community Group Presentations

Objective

To help staff identify and connect with community resources.

In ongoing efforts to connect school with the community, it is important to have representatives from outside agencies come into the school to share current resources and concerns. There is tremendous value in having an actual person from a community resource come to the school to engage in conversations and share challenges and strategies, and can also be beneficial to agency staff.

Time Required

15–20 minutes

Materials Needed

None

Instructions

Invite a representative from a community agency to visit during a staff meeting. Ask the representative to give a short presentation on how his or her community organization can help your school or program better fulfill its mission. For example, a representative from the public library can inform you of the youth activities the library offers and the latest reading trends of its younger patrons, or a parks and recreation worker can talk about seasonal park schedules and community sports. You can make this an ongoing component of staff meetings.

Community Publicity

Objective

To help staff connect with community resources.

A critical strategy for program success is to maintain and engage community support, and using existing systems is a good way to achieve that. This strategy requires ongoing communication with local media (newspapers, television network affiliates and cable channels, radio) to inform media of school or agency programs and school needs, but it can have high-impact rewards in terms of publicity and community awareness, engagement, and support.

Time Required

Ongoing

Materials Needed

Varies

Instructions

Appoint a staff person to serve as the main contact for local television and radio stations and newspapers, and have him or her regularly look for opportunities to let the local media know what's "going right" with your school or youth program. In addition, set aside time in each staff meeting for staff to suggest items that deserve recognition, and talk to staff regularly about connections they may have with local media. This strategy is also effective in the school setting. For example, set aside a time and date each week to recognize student and staff success (e.g., teams are doing well, individual student recognition, etc.).

Increasing Family Involvement

Objective

To help staff increase family involvement.

An ongoing challenge for staff is engaging and maintaining family support and involvement. Staff members can be reluctant to contact families with concerns because they fear a negative reception, but many families wish to be involved and would prefer early communication rather than notification after a negative pattern has been established. Using the power of "peer pressure" is a great strategy for any long-term challenge, in the same way that teaming up with a friend can keep you motivated in an exercise program.

Time Required

15 minutes once a week

Materials Needed

None

Instructions

Create peer groups for professional staff consisting of two to five members. Each member of the group sets a goal of making a set number of family contacts each week about positive student behaviors as well as student concerns. This group can also assist each other by acting as sounding boards and by brainstorming strategies for parent and student interventions. Teams check in once a week to compare results and discuss issues, and individual staff successes and challenges can be shared in full staff meetings if desired.

Student Recognition Program

Objective

To help staff connect with students and families.

The purpose of this activity is to recognize students who may not otherwise be recognized in any existing school program and to invite parents/families into the school community. The recognition program occurs twice a year and can be used for primary, junior high, or senior high schools. One urban high school used this activity, and in their first attempt staff nominated more than 80 students. More than 60 families attended the ceremony. This is a great and easy way to honor otherwise "unnoticed" youth.

Time Required

Nomination process: 15 minutes

Recognition ceremony: 1 hour

Coordination of entire program: 10 hours

Materials Needed

Letter for staff

Nomination forms

Letter for parents

Instructions

Send a letter to staff members explaining the student recognition program and ask them to fill out a nomination form for one or two students. They can nominate students "who demonstrate a positive attitude and show significant improvement in various areas of classroom work, service, and leadership." The recognition is not based on GPA and can be related to any department or classroom.

When you've collected the nominations, send a letter to the parents/guardians of youth who have been selected and invite them to the recognition ceremony. Then hold a brief ceremony (an hour long) for parents and recipients right after school. Include an address by the principal, presentation of certificates to students by the nominating teachers, and appropriate refreshments.

Student Recognition Program:
Letter for staff

Purpose
To recognize students who may not otherwise be recognized in any existing school program.

How do we do this?
Think of one or two students about whom you could say something positive. Staff members nominate students. Parents are invited to a recognition ceremony.

What are they being recognized for?
As the letter to parents will state, the purpose of the Student Recognition Award is to "recognize students who demonstrate a positive attitude and show significant improvement in various areas of classroom work, service, and leadership." This recognition is not based on GPA and can be related to any department or classroom.

What does the recognition look like?
A brief ceremony (one hour) for parents and recipients will include an address by the principal, presentation of certificates to students by the nominating teachers, and refreshments.

Tentative date:

If you have any questions, please contact:

Student Recognition Program: Nomination Form

For growth in the areas of leadership, participation in class, commitment, hard work, and/or attitude.

Teacher/staff person:

Student you are nominating:

Name of class student is in:

Grade: 9   10   11   12

Reason you are nominating this student:

A certificate will be prepared for you to present to the student, along with a few words from you.

Please return completed form to staff in charge by [date]:

Thank you

Example of letter for families

[Date]

[First Name] [Last Name]

[Address]

Dear Parents/Guardians of [youth],

Your child has been selected to receive a Student Recognition Award. The purpose of this award is to recognize students who demonstrate a positive attitude and show significant improvement in various areas of classroom work, service, and leadership.

The selection was made by [staff member], [connection to youth].

You are invited to attend a recognition ceremony and reception in honor of all award recipients on [date] in [place] at [time].

Congratulations to your family on [youth]'s fine achievement.

Sincerely,

Asset Category Handouts

Objective

To help staff understand Developmental Assets.

These materials provide tools for staff to review key concepts introduced in the PowerPoint presentation about the Developmental Assets (see Chapter 3). They will help staff deepen their knowledge and review concrete examples of asset building that they can use. These tools can serve as quick visual and written reminders and promote simple asset-building actions.

Time Required

Minimal, but requires regular attention

Materials Needed

Asset Category handouts for all staff, distributed according to the calendar

Instructions

For each month of the school program year, a site leader will introduce a new category that will help reinforce and build asset awareness with staff. The following schedule assumes that you will spend one month on each asset category, thus taking a year to complete all eight asset categories. You can, however, spend two months on each asset category instead so that you go through all the asset categories in two years.

This plan employs "asset buddies" to give staff one-on-one time with each other to discuss the assets. You can assign asset buddies, have staff choose their own buddies, or draw them at random.

Month (school year)	Category Focus
	(This model assumes one category per month. Another option is to discuss one category every two months on a multiyear rotation.)
September	General introduction to Developmental Assets
October	Support asset category
November	Empowerment asset category
December	Boundaries and Expectations asset category
January	Constructive Use of Time asset category
February	Commitment to Learning asset category
March	Positive Values asset category
April	Social Competencies asset category
May	Positive Identity asset category

First Half Month (or Month):

1. Distribute the two handout pages associated with the relevant category to all staff members (either in their mailboxes or in person).

2. Request that staff read the handouts and be prepared to offer some reaction to them at the monthly staff meeting (or first staff meeting of the month).

3. Select an asset-building idea from the specific affirmations for each category (see pages 118–125); write it on an index card titled *Start the day with this thought*. E-mail to staff or distribute to staff members as they check their mailboxes for the day. (See below for additional ideas on using affirmations.)

Second Half Month (or Month):

1. Have asset buddies follow up on the handout pages; ask them to have a short conversation about any aspect of the handout they would like to discuss.

   You might ask:

   - What stood out for you as you read the handout?

   - Do you have any questions about this category of assets? What are your thoughts about this category?

   - Which of the ideas for building assets have you implemented in an intentional way during the past few weeks? (Note: Staff members may have their own ideas.)

   - What is going well for you?

   - Have you encountered any challenges? To what do you attribute these challenges?

   - How have your students responded?

2. Ask the buddies to record ideas, quotes, and so on that might be helpful for other staff in the future.

3. Find ways of celebrating and acknowledging efforts privately and publicly.

An Introduction to Developmental Assets®

Why do some young people grow up with ease, while others struggle? Why do some youth get involved in dangerous activities, while others spend their time contributing to society in positive ways? Why do some youth "beat the odds" in difficult situations, while others get trapped?

Many factors—economic circumstances, family dynamics, genetics, traumatic events—shape young people's lives and choices. Research by Search Institute has identified 40 concrete, positive experiences and qualities—called Developmental Assets—that have a tremendous influence on young people's lives. The assets are grouped in eight categories.

The 40 Developmental Assets represent everyday wisdom about positive experiences that young people need. These assets help make it less likely that young people will get involved in problem behaviors. They also make it more likely that young people will engage in positive behaviors. This "power of the assets" is evident across all cultural and socioeconomic groups of youth.

THE EIGHT CATEGORIES OF DEVELOPMENTAL ASSETS

EXTERNAL ASSETS

1. **Support**—Young people need to experience the presence, care, help, and love of their families and many others. They need organizations and institutions that provide positive, nurturing environments.

2. **Empowerment**—Young people need to be valued by their community and have opportunities to contribute to others. For this to occur, they must be safe and feel secure.

3. **Boundaries and Expectations**—Young people need to know what is expected of them and whether activities and behaviors are "in bounds" or "out of bounds."

4. **Constructive Use of Time**—Young people need constructive, enriching opportunities for growth through creative activities, youth programs, congregational involvement, and quality time at home.

INTERNAL ASSETS

5. **Commitment to Learning**—Young people need to develop a lifelong commitment to education and learning.

6. **Positive Values**—Youth need to develop strong values that guide their choices.

7. **Social Competencies**—Young people need skills and competencies that equip them to make positive choices, build relationships, and succeed in life.

8. **Positive Identity**—Young people need a strong sense of their own power, purpose, worth, and promise.

What Are Developmental Assets? Essential building blocks for young people's successful growth and development.

THE MORE ASSETS YOUNG PEOPLE HAVE, THE BETTER

Assets have a powerful, positive effect on a young person. Assets promote actions that we hope for:

- Succeeding in school

- Helping others

- Maintaining good health

- Resisting danger

- Overcoming adversity

We know that the 40 assets also protect young people from making dangerous choices. Search Institute's data show that young people with more assets are less likely to engage in risky behaviors, including:

- Use of alcohol and other drugs

- Sexual intercourse

- Violent acts

- Gambling

In addition, young people with more assets are less likely to have eating disorders, or to be depressed, or to commit suicide.

MOST YOUNG PEOPLE DON'T HAVE ENOUGH ASSETS

Based on Search Institute's survey of more than 2 million students in grades 6–12, these are the percentages of youth who report each level of assets:

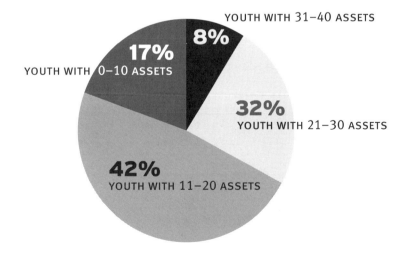

Asset Category 1: Support
Creating Caring Relationships

Support is important for everyone, young or older. We like knowing who will be there for us and whom we can count on. We enjoy the company of those who make us laugh, who make us think, who help us sort through tough issues. Support is not only the glue that holds people together but also the glue that keeps us together on the inside.

Yet, in a hectic society with so many demands, we sometimes forget the importance of noticing and connecting with one another. The result is that too many young people (and adults) feel isolated and alone.

The framework of Developmental Assets includes six Support assets that have a significant impact on the way young people grow up.

THE SIX SUPPORT ASSETS

1. **Family Support**—Family life provides high levels of love and support.

2. **Positive Family Communication**—Young person and her or his parent(s) communicate positively, and young person is willing to seek advice and counsel from parent(s).

3. **Other Adult Relationships**—Young person receives support from three or more nonparent adults.

4. **Caring Neighborhood**—Young person experiences caring neighbors.

5. **Caring School Climate**—School provides a caring, encouraging environment.

6. **Parent Involvement in Schooling**—Parent(s) are actively involved in helping young person succeed in school.

Supportive relationships provide the conduit for all other asset building.

What Is Support?
Young people need to experience the presence, care, help, and love of their families and many others. They need organizations and institutions that provide positive, nurturing environments.

How Young People Experience Support

WHAT'S SUPPORTIVE?

According to researchers, those who are best at determining what is supportive are those who receive support, not those who give it!

THE SUPPORT ASSETS—WHAT WE'VE LEARNED

The six Support assets are essential in providing a solid foundation for children and teenagers. Based on Search Institute's surveys of almost 150,000 students in 202 communities, the following percentages of young people report experiencing these assets:

ASSET 1. FAMILY SUPPORT — 68%

ASSET 2. POSITIVE FAMILY COMMUNICATION — 28%

ASSET 3. OTHER ADULT RELATIONSHIPS — 43%

ASSET 4. CARING NEIGHBORHOOD — 37%

ASSET 5. CARING SCHOOL CLIMATE — 29%

ASSET 6. PARENT INVOLVEMENT IN SCHOOLING — 29%

IDEAS FOR BUILDING THE SUPPORT ASSETS

- Greet every participant with a smile— use his or her name!

- Think "support" verbally and nonverbally.

- Listen attentively.

- Find creative ways to celebrate participants' successes and help them deal with failures.

- Focus on developing long-term relationships and think about how to sustain them over time.

- Show up, be a cheerleader, participate at your program, and participate in other programs.

Take a Moment for Reflection: Ask Yourself

How am I connecting with my students?

How can I deepen my relationships with my students?

What do my students need that I can provide during the time we spend together?

Asset Category 2: Empowerment
A Chance to Contribute

The four Empowerment assets are about visions, dreams, and opportunities. When young people feel safe, serve others, and perceive that others value them, they take healthy risks and try new challenges.

Empowered young people feel good about themselves and their skills. They grow up feeling respected and with a sense that they can make a difference in the world. Empowered youth are given opportunities to contribute to society in meaningful ways.

THE FOUR EMPOWERMENT ASSETS

7. **Community Values Youth**—Young person perceives that adults in the community value youth.

8. **Youth as Resources**—Young people are given useful roles in the community.

9. **Service to Others**—Young person serves in the community one hour or more per week.

10. **Safety**—Young person feels safe at home, at school, and in the neighborhood.

Service to Others is often called a gateway asset.

What Is Empowerment?
Young people need to be valued by their community and have opportunities to contribute to others. For this to occur, they must be safe and feel secure.

How Young People Experience Empowerment

THE EMPOWERMENT ASSETS–WHAT WE'VE LEARNED

The four Empowerment assets help us understand how valued young people feel. Based on Search Institute's surveys of almost 150,000 students in 202 communities, the following percentages of young people report experiencing these assets:

ASSET 7. COMMUNITY VALUES YOUTH   ▰▰▰▰▰ **22%**

ASSET 8. YOUTH AS RESOURCES   ▰▰▰▰▰ **26%**

ASSET 9. SERVICE TO OTHERS   ▰▰▰▰▰▰▰▰▰ **48%**

ASSET 10. SAFETY   ▰▰▰▰▰▰▰▰▰ **51%**

IDEAS FOR BUILDING THE EMPOWERMENT ASSETS

- Provide emotional safety by monitoring behavior, including bullying and put-downs.

- Encourage participant input and follow-through.

- Support participants in taking the lead in activities.

- Enlist youth in forming rules and consequences within the program.

- Provide opportunities for meaningful service—be creative, go beyond cleaning up.

> **Take a Moment for Reflection:**
> **Ask Yourself**
> How was I empowered as I grew up?
>
> How did being empowered make me feel?

Asset Category 3:
Boundaries and Expectations
Boundaries That Teach

Many people think of discipline when they look at the six Boundaries and Expectations assets. Yet, too often people think of discipline in negative terms and as punishment. The Latin word for discipline means both "to teach" and "to learn."

Teaching is what these assets are all about—teaching what's admirable and what's not, what's appropriate and what's inappropriate.

This category of assets also reminds us of the importance of consistency. Young people benefit from hearing the same messages about what's in bounds and out of bounds from parents, school, and the community at large.

THE SIX BOUNDARIES AND EXPECTATIONS ASSETS

11. **Family Boundaries**—Family has clear rules and consequences and monitors the young person's whereabouts.

12. **School Boundaries**—School provides clear rules and consequences.

13. **Neighborhood Boundaries**—Neighbors take responsibility for monitoring young people's behavior.

14. **Adult Role Models**—Parent(s) and other adults model positive, responsible behavior.

15. **Positive Peer Influence**—Young person's best friends model responsible behavior.

16. **High Expectations**—Both parent(s) and teachers encourage the young person to do well.

ROLE MODELS ARE IMPORTANT

Young people need adults and peers who set standards and uphold them, acting in ways that are respectful and responsible, and who show them that some things are worth working and waiting for. Serving as a role model is one of the best ways to teach important values and social skills.

What Are the Boundaries and Expectations Assets?
Young people need to know what is expected of them and whether activities and behaviors are "in bounds" or "out of bounds."

How Young People Experience Boundaries and Expectations

THE BOUNDARIES AND EXPECTATIONS ASSETS— WHAT WE'VE LEARNED

The six Boundaries and Expectations assets provide young people with important information that keeps them safe and lets them stretch and grow. Based on Search Institute's surveys of almost 150,000 students in 202 communities, the following percentages of young people report experiencing these assets:

ASSET 11. FAMILY BOUNDARIES — **46%**

ASSET 12. SCHOOL BOUNDARIES — **52%**

ASSET 13. NEIGHBORHOOD BOUNDARIES — **47%**

ASSET 14. ADULT ROLE MODELS — **27%**

ASSET 15. POSITIVE PEER INFLUENCE — **63%**

ASSET 16. HIGH EXPECTATIONS — **48%**

IDEAS FOR BUILDING THE BOUNDARIES AND EXPECTATIONS ASSETS

- Provide clear rules and consistent consequences.

- Use positive strategies to affect behaviors—"catch" youth doing good things, provide positive reinforcement, redirect to new activities.

- Give incentives for good behavior— extra privileges, opportunities for special activities.

- Model respectful behavior.

- Enlist youth in modeling good boundaries for others.

- Tell youth directly that you have high expectations for them and be explicit about those expectations.

- Inspire youth: let them hear from older youth who are on the way to meeting admirable, achievable goals.

Take a Moment for Reflection: Ask Yourself

Which boundaries do I think are most important for kids today? Why?

What's my role in establishing and monitoring boundaries in my family, school, neighborhood, or organization?

What rules or boundaries do I live by?

Asset Category 4:
Constructive Use of Time
Time Well Spent

The four Constructive Use of Time assets show that *how* young people spend their time makes a big difference in the way they grow up. Involving youth in activities that provide structure is not just a nice thing to do, it is essential.

Ideally these activities are led by principled, caring adults who nurture and model skill and capacity through group activities, lessons, relationships, and supervision. Out-of-school activities can provide balance in the range of activities, **connections** (peer to peer and youth to adult), **challenges**, **safe places**, and **opportunities for growth**.

THE FOUR CONSTRUCTIVE USE OF TIME ASSETS

17. **Creative Activities**—Young person spends three or more hours per week in lessons or practice in music, theater, or other arts.

18. **Youth Programs**—Young person spends three or more hours per week in sports, clubs, or organizations at school and/or in the community.

19. **Religious Community**—Young person spends one or more hours per week in activities in a religious institution.

20. **Time at Home**—Young person is out with friends "with nothing special to do" two or fewer nights per week.

What Are the Constructive Use of Time Assets?

Young people need constructive, enriching opportunities for growth through creative activities, youth programs, congregational involvement, and quality time at home.

How Young People Experience Constructive Use of Time Assets

THE CONSTRUCTIVE USE OF TIME ASSETS—WHAT WE'VE LEARNED

Based on Search Institute's surveys of almost 150,000 students in 202 communities, the following percentages of young people report experiencing these assets:

ASSET 17. CREATIVE ACTIVITIES **21%**

ASSET 18. YOUTH PROGRAMS **57%**

ASSET 19. RELIGIOUS COMMUNITY **58%**

ASSET 20. TIME AT HOME **51%**

IDEAS FOR BUILDING THE CONSTRUCTIVE USE OF TIME ASSETS

- Provide a variety of activities within your own program.

- Look for opportunities for one-to-one interaction.

- Showcase participants' gifts and talents.

- Offer as many choices within your program as you can.

- Ask for participant input and use it as much as possible.

- Make it a point to tell parents what their children are involved in and what they are learning and accomplishing.

Take a Moment for Reflection: Ask Yourself

Which of the four Constructive Use of Time assets had the most impact on me when I was young?

How do I spend my time now? Where can I find time to build assets for and with young people?

Asset Category 5:
Commitment to Learning
Learning for a Lifetime

THE FIVE COMMITMENT TO LEARNING ASSETS

21. **Achievement Motivation**—Young person is motivated to do well in school.

22. **School Engagement**—Young person is actively engaged in learning.

23. **Homework**—Young person reports doing at least one hour of homework every school day.

24. **Bonding to School**—Young person cares about her or his school.

25. **Reading for Pleasure**—Young person reads for pleasure three or more hours per week.

A commitment to learning is a commitment to growing. When we learn something new, we grow, change, and expand our horizons. This is true whether one is age 2, 14, or 60. The Commitment to Learning assets are built for and with children and youth through adults' attitudes, encouragement, involvement, and modeling. Young people look to their teachers, parents, and neighbors to learn new information, ideas, and perspectives.

> **What Is Commitment to Learning?**
> Young people need to develop a lifelong commitment to both formal and informal education.

How Young People Experience the Commitment to Learning Assets

THE COMMITMENT TO LEARNING ASSETS: HOW THEY STACK UP

The five Commitment to Learning assets show how much young people are motivated to learn. Based on Search Institute's surveys of almost 150,000 young people in 202 communities, the following percentages of young people report experiencing these assets:

ASSET 21. ACHIEVEMENT MOTIVATION — 65%

ASSET 22. SCHOOL ENGAGEMENT — 55%

ASSET 23. HOMEWORK — 47%

ASSET 24. BONDING TO SCHOOL — 52%

ASSET 25. READING FOR PLEASURE — 22%

IDEAS FOR BUILDING THE COMMITMENT TO LEARNING ASSETS

- Model curiosity and discovery. A commitment to learning is contagious.

- Read with young people and encourage them to read on their own.

- Make learning relevant. Young people benefit from seeing how learning applies to working.

- Highlight learning beyond the classroom. Learning happens in many different places—in homes, nature, community centers, congregations, workplaces, and parks.

Take a Moment for Reflection: Ask Yourself

When have I really enjoyed learning? Was it the subject matter, or the way I learned it?

If a student asked me why I thought everyone should read, what would I say?

Asset Category 6: Positive Values
Passing Along Positive Values

THE SIX POSITIVE VALUES ASSETS

26. **Caring**—Young person places high value on helping other people.

27. **Equality and Social Justice**—Young person places high value on promoting equality and reducing hunger and poverty.

28. **Integrity**—Young person acts on convictions and stands up for her or his beliefs.

29. **Honesty**—Young person "tells the truth even when it is not easy."

30. **Responsibility**—Young person accepts and takes personal responsibility.

31. **Restraint**—Young person believes it is important not to be sexually active or to use alcohol or other drugs.

You hear a lot of debate these days about values, but it's clear that our society needs to nurture worthwhile principles, standards, and qualities in children and young people to help make them strong. Values become an inner compass that young people can use to guide them in making choices in a confusing world. In 2007, Search Institute researchers surveyed parents about which topic they wanted to learn more about, and most parents (88 percent) chose "developing positive values" as their number one choice. It is also the job of each of us, not just schools.

While we may never agree on all the values that are important for young people, most people can agree on a few. The six Positive Values assets are one way of naming a set of positive principles, standards, and qualities that virtually everyone can affirm.

> **What Are Positive Values?**
> Young people need to develop strong values that shape their characters and guide their choices.

How Young People Experience the Positive Values Assets

THE POSITIVE VALUES ASSETS: HOW THEY STACK UP

The six Positive Values assets are at the core of what develops character in young people. Based on Search Institute's surveys of almost 150,000 young people in 202 communities, the following percentages of young people report experiencing these assets:

ASSET 26. CARING — 50%

ASSET 27. EQUALITY AND SOCIAL JUSTICE — 52%

ASSET 28. INTEGRITY — 68%

ASSET 29. HONESTY — 66%

ASSET 30. RESPONSIBILITY — 63%

ASSET 31. RESTRAINT — 45%

IDEAS FOR BUILDING THE POSITIVE VALUES ASSETS

- Model the Positive Values assets.

- Talk to people of all ages (young and older) in respectful ways.

- Discuss equality and social justice issues on a regular basis.

- Choose a cause for your students to follow, and support the work of those who are making progress in your area of concern.

- Develop easy ways for people of all ages in your school or program to contribute to worthy causes through their time, their talent, or their money.

Take a Moment for Reflection: Ask Yourself

Which value is the easiest for me to live out? What can I do to pass this value along to others in my family, neighborhood, school, organization, or community?

Which value is the most challenging to me? What can I do to make sure I'm modeling this value as much as possible for people in my life?

Asset Category 7: Social Competencies
Skills for Growing and Living

THE FIVE SOCIAL COMPETENCIES ASSETS

32. **Planning and Decision Making**—Young person knows how to plan ahead and make choices.

33. **Interpersonal Competence**—Young person has empathy, sensitivity, and friend-ship skills.

34. **Cultural Competence**—Young person has knowledge of and comfort with people of different cultural/racial/ethnic backgrounds.

35. **Resistance Skills**—Young person can resist negative peer pressure and dangerous situations.

36. **Peaceful Conflict Resolution**—Young person seeks to resolve conflict nonviolently.

Social competencies are the skills all people need to navigate successfully through life. Without social competencies, people lack the essential skills they need to live their values, contribute in meaning-ful ways, get along with others, and be responsible members of society.

> **What Are Social Competencies?**
> Young people need skills and com-petencies that equip them to make positive choices, build relationships, and succeed in life.

Learning social competencies is like learning how to play the piano. Rarely does the piano playing sound very good at first. Likewise, to develop basic skills needed for life we need "piano teachers" more than "music critics." We need suggestions for new methods to try and encouragement to keep going when we make mistakes. We need to be cheered on as we learn to master skills.

Young people especially need adults and peers who demonstrate, teach, and practice skills with them. They need adults and peers who watch how they are doing with their skills and who give them feedback along the way. They need people who not only teach them and show them the way, but also let them make and learn from mistakes.

How Young People Experience the Social Competencies Assets

THE SOCIAL COMPETENCIES ASSETS: HOW THEY STACK UP

The five Social Competencies assets encompass a number of skills young people need to succeed. Based on Search Institute's surveys of almost 150,000 young people in 202 communities, the following percentages of young people report experiencing these assets:

ASSET 32. PLANNING AND DECISION MAKING **29%**

ASSET 33. INTERPERSONAL COMPETENCE **45%**

ASSET 34. CULTURAL COMPETENCE **43%**

ASSET 35. RESISTANCE SKILLS **41%**

ASSET 36. PEACEFUL CONFLICT RESOLUTION **40%**

IDEAS FOR BUILDING THE SOCIAL COMPETENCIES ASSETS

- Encourage students to share cultural customs and rituals from their heritage.

- Model good manners and expect good manners from your students.

- Have students identify a long-term goal and outline the steps they need to take to reach it.

- Think about ways you can involve young people in your organization's planning and decision-making agendas.

- Think about how well you already do with the five Social Competencies assets. Rate your own social competencies on a scale of 1 (not well at all) to 5 (very well). Underneath each asset, jot down one or two things you'll start doing to nurture it.

Take a Moment for Reflection: Ask Yourself
Why is it so important for people to be socially competent?

Who built my Social Competencies assets during my childhood and/or adolescence?

Asset Category 8: Positive Identity
Power, Purpose, and Promise

THE FOUR POSITIVE IDENTITY ASSETS

37. **Personal Power**—Young person feels he or she has control over "things that happen to me."

38. **Self-Esteem**—Young person reports having a high self-esteem.

39. **Sense of Purpose**—Young person reports that "my life has a purpose."

40. **Positive View of Personal Future**—Young person is optimistic about her or his personal future.

When young people sense their own power, purpose, worth, and promise, they can do just about anything they decide to do. The Positive Identity assets tie in closely with the Support assets. Young people who feel loved, supported, and nurtured are more apt to feel good about themselves and have a positive view of their future. Children and youth who have families, neighbors, friends, educators, and community residents who see the best in them are more likely to bring out the best in themselves and in those around them.

> **What Is Positive Identity?**
> Young people need a strong sense of their own power, purpose, worth, and promise.

How Young People Experience the Positive Identity Assets

THE POSITIVE IDENTITY ASSETS: HOW THEY STACK UP

The four Positive Identity assets indicate how young people feel about who they are and who they are becoming. Based on Search Institute's surveys of almost 150,000 young people in 202 communities, the following percentages of young people report experiencing these assets:

ASSET 37. PERSONAL POWER — 42%

ASSET 38. SELF-ESTEEM — 48%

ASSET 39. SENSE OF PURPOSE — 57%

ASSET 40. POSITIVE VIEW OF PERSONAL FUTURE — 72%

IDEAS FOR BUILDING THE POSITIVE IDENTITY ASSETS

- Show your students that you notice their individual talents and appreciate them.

- Never pass up an opportunity to be encouraging.

- Talk about plans for the future: ask students where they see themselves in five years . . . in ten years.

- When your students face difficulties, help them think through and act on solutions.

- Talk about the things that give your life a sense of purpose. Ask others what gives their life purpose.

- Build opportunities for self-expression into homework assignments.

Take a Moment for Reflection: Ask Yourself

Who nurtured my positive identity when I was younger?

How do I nurture that sense today?

Wallet Cards

Placing messages and reminders in a variety of places is another way to reinforce the behavior changes you seek in staff, and varying the messages on a weekly or monthly basis keeps the messages from becoming "stale."

The following messages are designed to be printed out, folded in half, and laminated to create wallet cards (you'll find ready-to-print versions on the accompanying CD-ROM). You can also use just the back design and put it on the back of staff ID badges. You can distribute all of them at once, giving different versions to different staff members and then having them trade cards during staff meetings, or hand out a new card each month to everyone. Changing or trading the cards will keep the messages fresh.

I WILL... Say good morning, good afternoon, and good evening • Be real! • Give my all • Do my best to help • Make time to talk • Be the kind of role model I would admire • Go beyond a "hello" • Make a difference • Interact with students and provide support whenever they need it • Be an example of caring and responsibility • Listen so they feel heard • • •

·········· FOLD ··········

I WILL...
MAKE A PERSONAL COMMITMENT TO
MAKE A DIFFERENCE WITH YOUNG PEOPLE

FOCUS ON ASSET-BUILDING ATTITUDE

I WILL... Learn young people's names • Respect all students' values and ideas • Take time to get to know those in my class • Give a high five to every kid I encounter each day • Do fun and engaging activities so that kids learn and progress • Strengthen communication skills so we better understand each other • Focus on building a sense of purpose and stronger self-esteem in each child • • • • • • • • • • •

·········· FOLD ··········

I WILL...
MAKE A PERSONAL COMMITMENT TO
MAKE A DIFFERENCE WITH YOUNG PEOPLE

FOCUS ON ASSET-BUILDING CONNECTIONS

I WILL... Create a challenging and flexible curriculum • Hook them on science • Spark students' interest in particular areas • Expand awareness of vocational opportunities • Direct my curriculum to both the students and the parents • Provide young people with training and experiences so they can become resources • Incorporate an asset-building activity each day • Make sure we communicate high expectations and support • • • • • • • •

·········· FOLD ··········

I WILL...
MAKE A PERSONAL COMMITMENT TO
MAKE A DIFFERENCE WITH YOUNG PEOPLE

FOCUS ON ASSET-RICH CURRICULUM
& PROGRAMMING

I WILL... Get to know at least 10 students—their names and career interests • Be curious about what they like • Have conversations with young people about their families • Focus on understanding the young people's interests • Instill a college-going culture and achievement in their families • Focus on quality interactions—connections and conversations that build positive identity • •

·········· FOLD ··········

I WILL...
MAKE A PERSONAL COMMITMENT TO
MAKE A DIFFERENCE WITH YOUNG PEOPLE

FOCUS ON ASSET-RICH INTERACTIONS

I WILL... Challenge people to think outside the normal routine • Be consistent • Look closely at our work • Focus on creating other adult role models who build relationships with youth • Create an alumni newsletter • Stay connected to young people over time • Recruit asset-rich volunteers to build strong relationships with students • Focus on community building • • • • • • • • • • • •

·········· FOLD ··········

I WILL...
MAKE A PERSONAL COMMITMENT TO
MAKE A DIFFERENCE WITH YOUNG PEOPLE

FOCUS ON ASSET-RICH ENVIRONMENT
FOR LEARNING AND GROWTH

Posters

The CD-ROM included with this book also contains five 11 x 17-inch posters that connect to the messages found on the wallet cards. You can print them out and post them in the staff lounge, break room, copy room, or any other place where staff will see them on a regular basis. You can also post them in public areas like hallways and the cafeteria if you would like students to see the messages too.

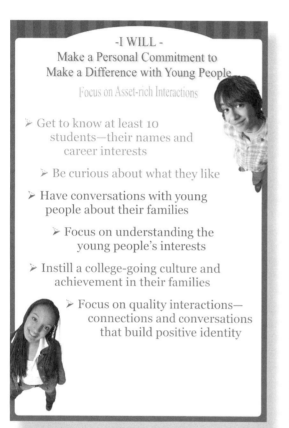

- I WILL -
Make a Personal Commitment to Make a Difference with Young People
Focus on Asset-rich Curriculum & Programming

➢ Create a challenging and flexible curriculum

➢ Hook them on science

➢ Spark students' interest in particular areas

➢ Expand awareness of vocational opportunities

➢ Direct my curriculum to both the students and the parents

➢ Provide young people with training and experiences so they can become resources

➢ Incorporate an asset-building activity each day

➢ Make sure we communicate high expectations and support

- I WILL -
Make a Personal Commitment to Make a Difference with Young People
Focus on Asset-building Attitude

➢ Say good morning, good afternoon, and good evening

➢ Be real!   ➢ Give my all

➢ Do my best to help

➢ Make time to talk

➢ Be the kind of role model I would admire

➢ Go beyond a "hello"

➢ Make a difference

➢ Interact with students and provide support whenever they need it

➢ Be an example of caring and responsibility

➢ Listen so they feel heard

- I WILL -
Make a Personal Commitment to Make a Difference with Young People
Focus on Asset-building Connections

➢ Learn young people's names

➢ Respect all students' values and ideas

➢ Take time to get to know those in my class

➢ Give a high five to every kid I encounter each day

➢ Do fun and engaging activities so that kids learn and progress

➢ Strengthen communication skills so we better understand each other

➢ Focus on building a sense of purpose and stronger self-esteem in each child

PUTTING IT ALL TOGETHER

Chapter 6

An Example of a Staff Development Plan

Chapter 6 suggests groupings for the materials we've provided and a sample schedule for putting everything together to create a cohesive asset-building program. You will be able to see how the print materials we suggested might be linked to meeting activities and other resources to help staff deepen their thinking about the Developmental Assets and the behaviors they want to use in their everyday practice.

This sample plan puts the components together in a way that reinforces the asset message and at the same time keeps it fresh. We also provide an example of calendar pages to help you visualize how you might build out your plan.

Staff Development Resources: Group 1

Miniposter: "Connections"

To be posted where staff can see it. Make as many copies as you wish.

Wallet card: "Connections"

Serves as an ongoing reminder of the personal commitments staff make as asset builders. Laminate and punch to clip to name badge lanyard, or use as wallet card.

Asset category: Support

Distribute the Support handout from Chapter 5 at a staff meeting and remind staff that the focus will be on the six Support assets.

E-mail messages:

- Reminder of library of asset materials and their location and checkout procedures.

- Reminder to staff members to connect with their asset buddies and discuss strategies for building relationships with students and with each other as staff.

Affirmations (select from the following):

- I know and use young people's names when I see them.

- Each day I greet young people warmly.

- Each day I am involved in spontaneous acts of asset building.

Reflection questions (select from the following):

- How am I connecting to youth?

- Are there little ways I could increase my connection to *more* students or *deepen* the connections I have with my current students?

- What is one thing from the "Connections" wallet card that I can do today or this week?

- What is one thing from the "Connections" wallet card that I will try to observe in others?

- How did I do this week in following through on my personal commitment to make asset-building connections?

- What is one relationship-building idea that I learned from observing or speaking with others?

Staff Development Resources: Group 2

Miniposter: "Interactions"

To be posted where staff can see it. Make as many copies as you wish.

Wallet card: "Interactions"

Serves as an ongoing reminder of the personal commitments staff make as asset builders. Laminate and punch to clip to name badge lanyard, or use as wallet card.

Asset category: Empowerment

Distribute the Empowerment handout from Chapter 5 at a staff meeting and remind staff that the focus will be on the four Empowerment assets.

E-mail messages:

- Reminder of library of asset materials and their location and checkout procedures.

- Reminder to staff members to connect with their asset buddies and discuss strategies for empowering students and each other as staff.

Affirmations (select from the following):

- I focus daily on young people's gifts and talents.

- I help young people focus on their strengths to overcome their deficits.

- When young people are in trouble, I begin my interactions with them by focusing on their strengths.

- I am expanding my asset building by pursuing relationships with young people I don't know.

Reflection questions (select from any of the following):

- How am I deepening my interactions with young people (the quality of the relationship, the interaction, connection over time, connection in other contexts)?

- How can I formalize a plan to build specific assets?

- What is one thing from the "Interactions" wallet card that I can do today or this week?

- What is one thing from the "Interactions" wallet card that I will try to observe in others?

- How did I do this week in following through on my personal commitment to make asset-building connections?

- What is one relationship-building idea that I learned from observing or speaking with others?

Staff Development Resources: Group 3

Miniposter: "Environment"
To be posted where staff can see it. Make as many copies as you wish.

Wallet card: "Environment"
Serves as an ongoing reminder of the personal commitments staff make as asset builders. Laminate and punch to clip to name badge lanyard, or use as wallet card.

Asset category: Boundaries and Expectations
Distribute the Boundaries and Expectations handout from Chapter 5 at a staff meeting and remind staff that the focus will be on the six Boundaries and Expectations assets.

E-mail messages:

- Reminder of library of asset materials and their location and checkout procedures.

- Reminder to staff members to connect with their asset buddies and discuss strategies for setting high expectations and appropriate boundaries for youth and for each other as staff.

Affirmations (select from the following):

- I encourage my fellow staff members and volunteers to build assets for and with youth and their families.

- I set high expectations for myself, fellow staff members, volunteers, and young people.

- I will learn and grow. Things can always get better; improvement is a process.

- I value experimenting—integrating a new way of being and doing. Seeing and influencing will take time and experimentation.

- I will commit to reflective practice and creating synergy among all those at my workplace.

Reflection questions (select from the following):

- Am I developing (learning and growing) as an intentional asset builder?

- How could I increase my knowledge and skills to be consistently asset based and developmentally attentive?

- What is one thing from the "Environment" wallet card that I can do today or this week?

- What is one thing from the "Environment" wallet card that I can discuss with a colleague?

Staff Development Resources: Group 4

Miniposter: "Curriculum and Planning"
To be posted where staff can see it. Make as many copies as you wish.

Wallet card: "Curriculum and Planning"
Serves as an ongoing reminder of the personal commitments staff make as asset builders. Laminate and punch to clip to name badge lanyard, or use as wallet card.

Asset category: Constructive Use of Time
Distribute the Constructive Use of Time handout from Chapter 5 at a staff meeting and remind staff that the focus will be on the four Constructive Use of Time assets.

E-mail messages:

- Reminder of library of asset materials and their location and checkout procedures.

- Reminder to staff members to connect with their asset buddies and discuss strategies for encouraging constructive use of time by youth and each other.

Affirmations (select from the following):

- I will provide high-quality activities that are engaging and allow for youth leadership and decision making.

- I will be enthusiastic about the activities I introduce and will communicate their value and importance.

- I will strive to ensure that each young person has a degree of success and accomplishment in each activity.

- I will encourage asset-rich peer relationships by creating safe and fun ways for students to help, teach, and cooperate and share ideas with each other.

Reflection questions (select from the following):

- How is the curriculum and programming I am involved in already asset-rich?

- Where are asset-building opportunities or places we could be more intentional in our curriculum or activities with students?

- What is one thing from the "Curriculum and Programming" wallet card I can do today or this week?

- What is one thing from the "Curriculum and Programming" wallet card I will try to observe in others?

- How did I do this week in following through on my personal commitment to focus on delivering an asset-rich curriculum and program activities?

- What examples of asset-rich curriculum were evident to me?

Sample Staff Development Calendar

Staff Development

- Introduce asset concept(s), build awareness
- Reinforce asset focus and emphasis
- Deepen asset-building knowledge, skills, attitudes

	WEEK 1	WEEK 2	WEEK 3
"I Will" wallet cards		Hand out first wallet card. Explain that these are a reminder and are connected to the poster.	
"I Will" miniposters	Hang first poster in staff areas		
Asset affirmations			
Asset reflection questions			
Staff meeting: (conversation starters, activities)	Staff meeting: Distribute "Support" handout and discuss		Staff meeting: Do "Rare Birds" activity
Other: Buddy system		Have staff select asset buddies	E-mail reminder: Check in with asset buddy and talk about positive and negative relationship strategies with students (from Group 1 resource list)
Other: Access to asset library	E-mail reminder: Checkout procedures		
Other:			

WEEK 4	WEEK 5	WEEK 6	WEEK 7	WEEK 8
		Hand out second wallet card. Explain that these are a reminder and are connected to the poster.		
	Hang second poster in staff areas			
E-mail reminder: Observe each other building relationships (from Group 1 reflection questions)		E-mail reminder: Bring one observation of asset building to staff meeting to celebrate		
	Staff meeting: Distribute "Empowerment" handout and discuss		Staff meeting: Do "Building Connections" activity	
				E-mail reminder: Buddies review their wallet cards and see what actions they have taken (from Group 2 resource list)
	E-mail reminder: Checkout procedures			

Supplemental Resources

If you have been using these activities and collateral materials with your staff, by now you have found ways to create time and space for conversation and reflection, and you are probably beginning to see changes in the ways staff are connecting to young people—and perhaps to each other. You may also be looking for ways to extend this work further. These additional resources from Search Institute provide you with tools you can use.

If you are working in a school setting, the following books, videos, and trainings can guide and support your efforts:

- *Great Places to Learn: Creating Asset-Building Schools that Help Students Succeed* uses the research on more than two million young people to explain how Developmental Assets help foster academic achievement and a healthy school climate.

- *A Quick-Start Guide to Building Assets in Your School: Moving from Incidental to Intentional* offers short sections with many suggestions and self-reflection questions.

- *Powerful Teaching: Developmental Assets in Curriculum and Instruction* includes chapters written by content specialists. Individual chapters can be purchased as downloadable PDFs.

- *Connecting in Your Classroom: 18 Teachers Tell How They Foster the Relationships that Lead to Student Success* contains stories and tips from teachers nominated as excellent at building connections with students.

If you are looking for more activities to use with staff, the activity books we have created for use with students have also been successfully used with adults:

- *The Best of Building Assets Together: Favorite Group Activities That Help Youth Succeed* contains 150 activities covering all of the Developmental Assets.

- *Pass It On at School! Activity Handouts for Creating Caring Schools* offers activities tailored to school settings.

- *Safe Places to Learn: 21 Lessons to Help Students Promote a Caring School Climate* builds attitudes and behaviors such as kindness, respect, and caring.

- *Ideas for Educators: 42 Ready-To-Use Newsletters for School Success* gives teachers tips for incorporating each asset into their work with students.

- *Instant Assets: 52 Short and Simple E-Mails for Sharing the Asset Message* offers short messages about each of the assets and asset categories, and the icons for the eight asset categories.

You can also book any of the following Search Institute trainings provided by Search Institute Training & Speaking (found on the Web at www.search-institute.org/training-speaking):

- Building Developmental Assets in School Communities

- Deepening Asset Building in School Communities

- Powerful Teaching: Adding Impact without Added Work

And two additional trainings from Search Institute Training & Speaking can also help you deepen asset-building attitudes and behaviors among staff:

- More than Just a Place to Go: Using Developmental Assets to Strengthen Your Youth-Serving Program

- Infusing Assets into Your Organization.

If you provide out-of-school programming for young people, the following resources will also be useful:

- *More than Just a Place to Go: How Developmental Assets Can Strengthen Your Youth Program* (book and DVD) shares examples of how and why to focus on strengthening relationships, environments, and programs to increase your impact on young people's healthy development.

- All of the activity books mentioned in the preceding pages can also be used in youth program settings and with youth program staff.

Search Institute continues to develop posters, self-adhesive notes, books, and other resources, so check the online store for additional resources you can use.

Index

About the Authors

Angela Jerabek, MS, has been working in public schools for 20 years. She developed the Building Assets, Reducing Risks (BARR) Program to address academic failure, truancy, discipline, school climate, and chemical use in schools using the Developmental Assets as its foundation. The BARR Program received a 2005 National Exemplary Prevention Program Award and has been listed in the National Registry of Evidence-Based Programs and Practices since 2009. It is being implemented in schools across the country. Angela was named a Champion of Health by Blue Cross Blue Shield and received a commendation from the St. Louis Park (Minnesota) Police Department for her work with youth. Angela has presented at more than 60 conferences across the nation. Angela has a master of science degree in counseling and is a licensed K–12 teacher. She resides in Minneapolis, Minnesota, with her husband and two children.

Nancy Tellett-Royce is a senior consultant at Search Institute and has been on the institute staff for 12 years. She has worked with Healthy Communities • Healthy Youth initiatives and with large and small organizations to help them develop staff and volunteers who can embed asset-building strategies in their work. She has also chaired and currently sits on the executive committee of Children First, an asset-building initiative in St. Louis Park, Minnesota. She is the author of *Supporting Youth: How to Care, Communicate, and Connect in Meaningful Ways* and coauthor of *Engage Every Parent: Encouraging Families to Sign On, Show Up, and Make a Difference*, both published by Search Institute Press.

As director of the Career Center at Macalester College and senior academic adviser at the University of Minnesota, Nancy was responsible for managing staff development activities for her staff members over a period of 14 years.

Acknowledgments

We would like to thank Kristin Johnstad, senior consultant at Search Institute, for creating and testing many of the staff development activities discussed in this book. Kristin, Pat Seppanen, and Sandy Longfellow, along with research assistants Katie Streit and Sandy Vue, created a number of these activities while they were working with the New York City Asset Labs (a project of the YMCA of New York City); with the Tiger Woods Learning Center in Anaheim, California; and with Prepared 4 Life, an after-school program in Houston, Texas.

We want to acknowledge the innovative and dedicated staff of St. Louis Park High School in St. Louis Park, Minnesota. The leadership of the administration and the creativity of the staff and their commitment to student success has helped pioneer effective school reform strategies. The staff generously shared their ideas and activities for this book. A special thank you go to Arika Mareck, Barb Nelson, and Kari Schwietering for their time, patience, and vision.

We would also like to thank the many asset builders who over the years have committed to deepening their skills and knowledge in order to improve outcomes for children and youth. Their eagerness to learn and to hone their skills has led to this book.